CONTENTS

FOREWORD

For more than 30 years the English Speaking Board and many leaders in education have been urging that more attention should be paid to speaking, to those skills of direct speech which help constitute personality and the power of communication at least as much as do the skills of writing. The mode of academic study was commonly reading and writing. 'Don't talk' was the commonest injunction on the lips of the teacher. Only in primary schools and the higher reaches of education, in university seminar and tutorial, did one suddenly find that the power of coherent oral utterance was valued and expected. For the most part, secondary education sent forth a reticent scholar to face the noisy, verbal world of workplace, family and political action. We were tongue-tied in English almost as much as in the foreign languages we had studied for so long. No one can guess how different industrial relations, family life and our commercial existence might then have been had the values of enjoyed, clear, vivid speech been pursued more successfully in our schools.

As the educational world has widened the scope of teaching methods and the ways of recording and reporting student progress, a larger and larger premium has been placed on speech. Discussion, negotiation, oral exposition as well as drama and workshops have become more powerful tools of the teacher's trade. And many of the national forms of examination, assessment and profiling now require an oral element, or will do before the end of the decade.

This book by Christabel Burniston, so long a doughty warrior in the field, and her collaborator Dr John Parry is much to be welcomed. As we move towards a 16+ examination which may embrace 70% of the age group, and raise the educational leaving age to 18+ through the two-year Youth Training Scheme and a medley of full-time training in schools and further education, all leading to general or vocational qualifications, the ideas and techniques recommended here as the fruits of years of experience, will be sorely needed by teachers and students.

John Tomlinson
Director,
Institute of Education,
University of Warwick.

PREFACE TO TEACHERS

Now that GCSE officially recognises the importance of oral work in English teaching, every sixteen year old will have to speak and write to be awarded a basic qualification. This book recognises that self-expression is crucial to every individual – if GCSE encourages more discussion and articulate, thoughtful argument in classrooms, it will, belatedly, start giving many thousands of students an official challenge to find their own voices. Moreover there is now a marked trend in assessment, in schools and more particularly in colleges of further education, to make testing more practical and *oral*. This book should prove useful to lecturers in technical colleges who are concerned with transmission of skills and opinions in vocational courses. We hope that this book will help.

Many schools have encouraged constructive talking and drama from an early age. Many have seen both as dangerous and undisciplined. So, it is very hard to write recommendations when there are so many different speakers and non-speakers to advise, from the frozen, impersonal platform of a printed textbook. We hope that you will move freely through the book, picking out the exercises that seem most useful – we begin and end with discussion: we go through a whole range of skills, some elementary, some hard for professional speakers and actors. This is a resource book of exercises that assumes a need for training the speaker; some people, like athletes, are born eager to master a special skill, others are verbally unfit, overweight or hamstrung. Everybody needs to train – not just to be more persuasive, but to be more receptive, to listen well as much as to speak well. We need to check that our message and other people's have been received and understood.

Most studies of classroom teaching have shown that the teacher speaks for the vast majority of the time and the student is unlikely to speak more than a few sentences per lesson. Some students may contribute less than ten minutes' speech to a week's lessons, so the idea that they must all now give talks and enter discussion can be extremely frightening. There are very few adults who feel comfortable talking, on a prescribed subject, to thirty of their peers. So, we have started, in Chapter 1, with the assumption that many students will need coaxing to express their opinions. If this seems naive, it's worth citing a recent report which found that the one common factor in teenagers' running away from home or institutional care was their feeling that no one would listen to them. Even the most disruptive and the most docile students need a way of speaking for themselves, about what matters to them.

Like Chapter 1, Chapter 2 is set out in three stages, this time to show ways of giving and receiving information. Clarity and accuracy are crucial in many jobs and recognised in a very wide range of qualifications. Whatever level of skill a student may have reached, we have tried to provide an exhaustive set of tasks, from simple relaying of information to complex exposition.

Chapter 3 moves, as many of the exercises do, from the impersonal to the personal.

Once again, we don't expect a class to work through every exercise, but so many students think they have nothing to contribute when asked to demonstrate a skill, that a wide range of suggestions should help give them confidence – the students, in any oral exam, are the experts, and the examiners are the people to be instructed. For once, the student is the authority, at the centre of the exercise, and many are amazed to find they have experience which no previous exam has asked for or rewarded.

The second stage of Chapter 3 asks students to work on other people's experiences and communicate their skills. Finally, there is a chance for general discussion and what may not seem like an oral exercise at all – responding to a confidential reference for a job application. This does, however, demand that students work together on a practical task in exactly the sort of conversation and collaboration illustrated in the previous chapter. So, some students may need to work through the stages of both chapters before being able to tackle this 'adult' job: some may be able to discuss and benefit from it much more quickly.

'Discovering your voice' (Chapter 4) starts from the assumption that people can improve their breathing techniques and posture to speak more confidently and easily. There are plenty of keep-fit clubs and body-building studios, but almost no general guidance on how to keep your voice in good shape. The exercises emphasise how much different emotions can make a voice become warmer and colder. The advertisers who give us deeply reassuring voice-overs on TV commercials know this: the politicians who train themselves to sound more caring exploit this. Everyone can use what is often a strangled and limited voice to far greater effect – and the dramatic selection of unusually powerful poems at the end of the chapter gives plenty of material for a group to work on, in full voice.

Chapter 5 (on interviews) continues the theme that you are your own best audio-visual aid. There are detailed recommendations on interview techniques, but not just from the usual point of view – how to get a job. A large number of suggestions on how to interview people yourself should help students build confidence, develop many contacts and put themselves in other people's shoes. Different stages of the chapter will be appropriate to different levels of maturity and different ambitions, but there is, we hope, a variety of active exercises that will make students more self-aware.

Reading passages aloud (Chapter 6) can be a deadly experience for both reader and audience. By suggesting a number of approaches with extracts both taxing and enjoyable, we have tried to turn a chore into an art. There is a detailed analysis of the Catch-22 passage; some teachers may find this unnecessary, but again you have the chance to compare your own practice and take the most helpful suggestions from ours. This is not a prescriptive book – just the best package of materials and methods for oral work that we can assemble. As usual, some of the recipes will be easy for skilled cooks and hard for beginners, but we have set out the ingredients as precisely as possible. The final success of the menu depends on the taste of the teacher and class.

Chapter 7 (personal projects) draws on a wealth of experience with English Speaking Boards exams. Couldn't most students think up their own? Many can, but our experience is that a large number welcome support and suggestions – so here are, literally, hundreds.

Drama ('Dialogue in action' – Chapter 8) may appear a familiar area, or one that many teachers find alarmingly uncontrollable. A selection of different approaches, with less familiar extracts and, as with all chapters, a comprehensive bibliography at the back of the book, should encourage teachers and students to experiment and develop new ways of self-expression. Interviews, exam orals and all sorts of meetings require stage management, careful delivery of lines and precise movements, to concentrate your audience's attention on the points you particularly want them to appreciate.

Chapters 9 and 10 look at ways of protesting, formally debating and monitoring newspapers. These are all areas where reasoned and fluent argument can have great effect; some of these techniques are immediately relevant to exams (e.g. the discussion of news items) but all are important if a student is going to respond to the many pressures that sophisticated and professional users of language can exert.

At the end of the *GCSE English Guide for Teachers*, produced by the Secondary Examinations Council in collaboration with the Open University, the following twelve categories are indicated for oral assessment:

1	Content	7	To narrate
2	Delivery	8	To present a point of view
3	Appropriateness	9	To discuss a point of view
4	Reciprocity	10	To ask questions
5	Ability to transmit ideas and feelings	11	To answer questions
6	To describe experience	12	To describe a process

Nearly all these areas overlap, and failure or success in, say, appropriate speaking, will inevitably indicate a lot about delivery and reciprocity. We are very aware that many of the exercises in our book go to and fro over the same ground: that some are dauntingly ambitious and others apparently elementary; that we give a great deal of guidance at one point, a simple outline at the next. All speaking, however, combines complex and simple skills.

In the end, the fluency of your students will depend on the atmosphere you create in the classroom – too much checking and examining can effectively kill all spontaneity, too little can encourage drivel. We hope that the enormous range of material included in these chapters will give everybody scope to discover and develop direct speech.

1 Introductions

STAGE 1   Making connections

1 In a new group

If you've joined a new group, you need to know who they all are and they need to know something about you. It's very difficult to describe yourself to a group of strangers so you should introduce the person next to you, and he/she should introduce you.

■ *EXERCISE*

5 minutes maximum – work in pairs

a) Turn to the person on your right and establish their name; where they come from; why they're in this group; what do they want to get out of the course; what do they like best and least about – school; pop music; families; food; people; holidays; houses; jokes.

b) Don't rush through this list: the more your partner sounds interested in any one subject, encourage a longer discussion. You may have a very interesting five minutes on just one or two items.

c) Make a note of the main answers, particularly the person's name and interests.

d) At the end of the discussion, introduce your partner to the rest of the group with a polite, brief summary of what you found out.

e) Change over. Your partner will now interview you. Because the introductions are mutual, you should both help each other, rather than show off at the other person's expense. Everyone in the group should now feel much more at ease, because they know a little about each other and everyone has spoken constructively.

2 Your worst moment

You should now have the confidence to speak for yourself, but you might not want to speak in front of the whole group. So, talk to your partner at greater length about something that made a big impact on you – e.g. my first day at school; missing the last bus; the news item that made me sick; ex-friends; people who interfere; if I could make that decision again ...; a disastrous holiday; pet hates.

■ *EXERCISE*

5 minutes maximum – work in pairs

a) Describe what upset you and why, in as much detail as possible.

b) If you run out of things to say, let your partner know more about the background: what sort of people come into the story? (you may know them well, but your partner won't) what makes the incident stick in your mind? Do you feel as strongly now as when it happened? If you've changed in your feelings about it, why have you changed?

c) Feedback: your partner should say what he/she thinks about it and whether he/she would have been equally upset.

d) With your permission, your partner could tell the whole group what you've said and why the way you described your experience made a big impact. Or, you may now feel confident enough to talk to the whole group about your worst moment, directly. It's up to you to decide when you talk to a bigger audience than the partner you know. You may well want to have many more small-scale discussions, and try out the exercises in the different stages of this chapter, first.

What do you think the story is behind this?

3 It makes me angry

Another way of finding that you can speak forcibly is to give a short series of comments on a subject that makes you indignant. Make a list of points so you have five or six strong arguments to tell your partner – the whole talk should only last a minute. Here are some possible topics:

Personal members of the family who irritate you because they're bossy, nagging, noisy, bad at listening, bad at talking.

Social gossips, hypocrites, awkward customers and bosses, bad drivers, what the council does or doesn't do about your neighbourhood.

Institutional 'If I were in charge of this school/classroom/hospital/youth club/doctor's surgery/DHSS office/assembly/canteen etc., the first thing I'd change would be . . .'

Morals Do we have the right to: stockpile nuclear weapons while people starve? hunt foxes? experiment on animals to develop new medicines? hang murderers? help the old or terminally ill to commit suicide? abort unwanted or damaged babies?

■ *EXERCISE*

1 minute + up to 5 minutes follow-up discussion – work in pairs

a) Make your comments, as forcefully and clearly as you can, using your list of checkpoints.

b) Listen to your partner's comments on what you've said. Was there too much emotion, even though the case you put was sincere and easy to understand? Were all your arguments logical?

c) Ask your partner to say what he/she thinks about the issue, and comment on these thoughts.

d) Find out what the rest of the group chose as a topic. If several people chose similar ones, work in larger groups and compare how each person tackled the question and who made the most effective arguments.

4 Heroes

So far, there's been a stress on negative feelings. This is because it's nearly always easier to criticise than praise and, if you're not used to talking in unfamiliar groups, you expose less of yourself saying what doesn't appeal to you rather than what does. Once you start to gain confidence, though, it's important to try positive exercises, too. It's easy to be destructive and cynical: harder to be enthusiastic, but here's the reverse side of exercise 3. Simply make a list of people you admire from:

Personal knowledge; members of your family; neighbours; friends.
Social people who've done a lot for the community.
Institutional politicians; leaders of pressure groups; historical figures.
Sports and pop stars are they more important to you than anybody listed above? Why?

■ *EXERCISE*

1–5 minutes – work in groups of two or three

a) Simply read out your list of names, with a very brief comment on what you admire.

b) Develop this into an award ceremony for a New Year's Honours List – what prizes would you give each of your heroes and why?

c) *Jim'll Fix It*: Following the idea of Jimmy Saville's TV show, say what you'd most like to see your hero doing on television, with you helping, for a good cause.

d) Change round. Listen to your partner's list of heroes and see whether they've anything in common with your list.

e) As a group, you could see who comes out top in most people's lists and discuss why one or two people are general favourites, particularly if some of the group don't agree they are heroes.

(For 'heroes', please read 'and heroines' – it's just tedious to write both every time).

---

5 I believe

A final exercise to put a positive viewpoint.

☐ *EXERCISE*

5 minutes or longer – work in groups of two or three

a) Write down everything that you strongly believe about the way people should be treated (the old, the sick, the young, the handicapped, the poor, the rich, the terrorist, the rapist, the mugger, the mad, the people who have a religion different from yours, the people who have no religion, the opposite sex, people with different coloured skins, people with different sexual preferences, or any people with strong views different from your own).

b) Swop your list with your partner's and read it carefully.

c) Pick out the items on it you're strongly in agreement or disagreement with.

d) Comment on these, and then let your partner reply.

e) Discuss whether it's possible to reconcile people who have totally opposite views.

STAGE 2   Conversation

By the end of Stage 1 or because of your normal experience in English lessons, you should be well able to hold a conversation in class. Nevertheless, it's worth checking the way you talk and the way you listen.

1 Listening

☐ *EXERCISE*

10 minutes – work in groups of three

a) Divide into groups of three. Two people will talk, the other watch how they talk.

b) The talkers should choose a topic from Stage 1 or take the subject of the conversation from right outside English lessons: e.g. the last party/the next party; what she said to me in the dinner queue; what I'd do with £1 million; the best programme on TV; the best game in the world (the subject should interest both talkers!).

c) While the two talkers discuss their chosen topic, the observer should score each of these points, on a scale 0–5 (0 the lowest, negative score, 5 the highest, positive score).

Techniques for listeners

	Negative	*Positive*
POSITION:	Distant or aggressively near	Close and interested
BODY:	Tense or fidgeting	Alert and relaxed
EYES:	Looking away, cold	Looking at speaker, responsive
SMILES:	Rare or unexpected	Mirroring speaker, encouraging
GENERAL REACTIONS:	Blank or impatient	Encouraging with brief gestures, murmurs of sympathy

Techniques for talkers

	Negative	*Positive*
POSITION:	Too close or assertive	Close, not overpowering
BODY:	Wooden gestures or violent ones ...	Relaxed, spontaneous
EYES:	Staring, not engaging listener	Watching listener and checking response
SMILES:	To show superiority or malice	Appropriate
VOICE:	Too loud/soft/monotonous	Right volume, clear, varied
CONTENT:	Monologue, blocking responses	Dialogue, consulting listener and asking for response

d) When observer has 'scored' the conversation, he/she says, 'Freeze' and the two talkers hold their position exactly, as in a still photograph. The observer then comments on this – is it a good position for communicating or a bad one? After unfreezing, the observer tells the talkers their 'score'.

e) The talkers comment on this: they may feel, for instance, that they were doing a lot better than the score indicates – they weren't shouting or being violent, but making their points forcefully.

Possible problems: This may lead the talkers to be very self-conscious, overdoing gestures to send up the exercise. But, at least you will be conscious of how people often don't listen or pretend to, while their eyes and body language say otherwise. A video of a TV discussion may be easier to analyse. Or people in the group who like acting might improvise a scene for the whole group to watch and comment on. (See Chapter 8 for suggestions on improvisation: high and low status exercises bring out ways of dominating a conversation very well).

2 Counselling

■ *EXERCISE*

10 minutes - group of four

a) Read these two parallel scenes, preferably with students playing the parts. (A is the person wanting help, B is the counsellor)

Opening 1

A. I wonder if I could have a word . . . ?

B. (*sighs*) Oh yes. Come in. What is it?

A. Well, if you're busy, I'll just –

B. (*brisk*) No, no. (*Aggressively*) Come in. That's what I'm here for. What's the problem?

A. Er – I'm probably just making a fuss, But I –

B. (*interrupting*) Why? Why are you doing that?
(*No answer*) What's wrong? Mmm?

A. I'm . . . er . . . I don't know how to put this.

B. You look washed out. You've been going out too much. (*Forced*

Opening 2

A. I wonder if I could have a word . . . ?

B. Yes, sure, a word about . . .

A. Mmm, well, it's a bit difficult.

B. Mmm. Let's sit down.

A. Er – it's . . . I'm getting these headaches.

B. I'm sorry. Headaches?

A. More like migraines. I've got some pills but they just make me feel sick.

B. Migraines can be terrible. Did the pills help at all?

A. They did at first, but then the doctor said it was all to do with stress, and I'd got to sort out what was causing the stress. And I didn't think it was stress.

laugh) Late nights always catch up with you, you know.

A. I don't actually go out, much.

B. No, very sensible, exams coming up and all that. You may find it's a bit drab now, but when all your party-mad friends are failing, and you can go on to a good 'A' level course, you'll be glad you worked.

A. I'm finding work a bit hard . . .

B. What subjects are you doing? You're doing Maths, English, Chemistry, Geography, History and Home Economics, aren't you? That seems like a reasonable workload.

A. Oh.

B. Some people have a lot more to do than that – do you know what I've got to get through today . . .?

B. What do you think it is?

A. I've had a lot of trouble with work, not getting things done, teachers shouting at me, I can't take it when they shout, you know, it's like my Dad. Why don't they realise the more they yell, the worse I get. I mean, do you like people yelling at you?

B. No, I certainly don't.

A. Like this morning – my Mum wasn't there so my Dad starts on at me about getting breakfast for my brother and I don't see why . . .

b) Why do we learn a lot more about A's problems in the second extract? Why is the counsellor in the first extract getting no information from A?

c) Describe one person you find particularly easy to talk to and say why. Describe one person you find particularly difficult to talk to and say why.

d) What can you or your partner suggest to make communication with the difficult person easier?

3 Co-operative conversation

Communication between an authority and a person asking for advice is not the only place where conversations go wrong. Communication between equals can be just as clumsy.

■ *EXERCISE*

10 minutes – work in groups of four

a) Read the following parallel discussions, preferably aloud, with different students playing the parts in front of the whole group, or partners reading the extracts together

Collaboration?

Type 1 duologue	*Type 2 duologue*

A: We've got to arrange the next assembly.

B: What does that mean?

A: I suppose we have to stand up and do something . . .

B: I can't act. I could ask Derek –

A: He's so big-headed.

B: What about some music?

A: They had that last week.

B: That was classical stuff, I mean something decent.

A: Like what?

B: Queen.

A: I hate Queen.

B: I can't help that. Lots of people like Queen. That last album – have you heard it?

A: No and I don't want to. I mean, what are you going to do, stand up there and put on Queen for ten minutes?

B: Ten minutes!

A: That's right.

B: I thought it was just us making a couple of jokes or something and then the rest of the form could . . .

A: Could what?

B: Join in.

A: Join in what? Miming to some pathetic record?

B: OK, OK, what do you suggest?

A: Um . . . (*silence*)

C: We've got to arrange the next assembly.

D: How long have we been given?

C: Ten minutes.

D: Can we use as many people as we like?

C: I suppose so – as long as we get them organised. It'll need rehearsing.

D: Oh, you want to do a play?

C: Not necessarily. But even if it's just a few people speaking and singing, they'll need a running order. It'll have to be varied.

D: Should we have a theme?

C: We could – it's near Christmas.

D: Yes, but everyone's pretty tired of hearing about Christmas – what about parties?

C: You mean, have a party in the hall?

D: We could have one group acting a party, some music playing –

C: We could get Mark to bring his group.

D: Some people think it's great to get as drunk as possible at parties.

C: You mean we do a sort of guide to people you meet at parties – and who helps and who makes them a disaster?

b) Who is the most helpful person here? How does he or she incorporate suggestions and develop them?

c) Who is the least helpful person here? Why does he or she achieve nothing?

d) Take a similar situation (preferably a real one, not just for the sake of this exercise) and see how far you can plan in five minutes: e.g. an end of term concert; food for a family party; choosing a present for a difficult old lady; a shopping expedition.

4 Putting people down

In most conversations, the balance isn't equal, since one speaker knows more, can draw on more experience or use words more rapidly – but the other speaker may well have more common sense, more insight or more empathy. The next exercise starts with boasting and shows how easy and destructive it is to override or ignore the other person.

'Aren't you lucky to be able to wear cheap clothes?'

□ *EXERCISE*

10 minutes – work in groups of two

a) Read this scene then continue it, either writing down the dialogue or improvising it aloud: one person plays E, one person plays F.

E: I've just got back from my holidays in the Bahamas.
F: I find the Bahamas frightfully expensive. Have you tried Mustique?
E: Three years ago, but it was overrun with photographers.
F: I think you'll find it's settled down quite a bit since then. We had a glorious time in June –
E: Far too hot in June. It's a draining heat, with my sensitive skin.
F: I've found this really excellent suncream. I've had to order it specially from New York, but my doctor said that it was vital for someone with such unusually delicate skin.
E: I'm allergic to cream. It's terribly messy ... (etc.)

b) In groups of three, now have an observer to score what the two talkers were saying. Each time one makes a claim that establishes how much better he or she is, give that person a point. Add up the score at the end – if the talkers are very good at putting each other down, you may need two scorers to keep up!

c) Discuss the scores. Do the talkers agree with the final count? What did they feel were the most rude or decisive remarks?

---

5 Building people up

☐ *EXERCISE*

Continuing 4 or to be used separately: 10 minutes – groups of two

a) Choose a subject where you feel nervous or unhappy about speaking out: e.g. in a shop asking for help with a very technical problem you don't understand (servicing a hi-fi, repairing a bicycle, using a computer attachment) or making a complaint to an official (at the Town Hall, Police Station, DHSS, etc.) or asking for medical advice.

b) Agree with your partner what the request consists of. Make a list of the points you want to get across.

c) Decide what are the most helpful ways the shop assistant or official could answer them.

STAGE 3   Informal discussions

You should now have enough practice with talking in twos and threes to feel that the prospect of talking in a larger group isn't so daunting. Points to remember:

1 Is everybody listening to each other?

We get so used to hearing a constant background of noise that we tend to treat people like TV broadcasts – unless they make a very big noise, we ignore them.

■ *EXERCISE*

Individual project for home or school followed by reporting back to group

Either:

a) Time the speeches in a soap opera like *Coronation Street* or *EastEnders*:

b) How many times did somebody interrupt? Not listen? Talk over somebody else's speech?

c) How many minutes had no background noise (traffic, music on radio or TV, pub sounds, etc.)?

Or:

d) Count how many times during a school day teachers tell you to be quiet, pay attention or listen to somebody: can you see a pattern to these commands (e.g. are classes noisier at the end of the day, during bad weather, in certain moods)?

2 Is everybody able to see and hear each other?

☐ *EXERCISE*

Discussion followed by review of what happened – work in groups of at least five

a) Choose one of the topics in this chapter and discuss it in the following groups:

    1) Everyone sitting in a circle
    2) Everyone sitting where he/she likes
    3) Everyone sitting in rows

b) How many more people felt able to take part in the first arrangement than the second?

c) Why do discussions work differently when people are arranged differently?

---

3 Is there a clear structure to the discussion?

☐ *EXERCISE*

Discussion followed by review of what happened – the whole class

a) Discuss whether school uniform is a positive feature of schools with the teacher acting as chairman – reminding you of the time limit on discussion; pointing out that uniform often gives a stronger sense of identity, equality and pride in the school; limiting all contributions to the discussion to thirty seconds. (*Approx: 5 minutes*)

b) Discuss this topic: 'What's the one rule that must be obeyed by everyone if a school is to function?': there should be no chairman, no intervention by the teacher, no mention of time (though the teacher will halt the discussion after five minutes), no rules about how long anyone can speak for.

c) Compare the two discussions: they are obviously extremes, and you should try out versions which are different from your normal practice in class, to decide the answers to these questions (*not more than 5 minutes*):

Time: should discussion be open-ended or do deadlines help you?
Chairman: does he/she hinder or help the group?
Topics: how clearly should they be defined at the start?
Personalities: which system helped most people speak and think?

Open-mindedness: how many people made concessions?
Conclusion: did anybody feel differently at the end or would a vote then
  have produced the same results as one at the start?

---

4 Monitoring the discussion

Now you have decided the best way to organise the discussion, have one
person in each group act as observer. These observers should inconspicuously
mark up the following chart to see which speakers are constructive and which
overpowering or apathetic. As it's difficult to monitor more than four people at
a time, either have small-group discussions (which you may have decided are
more productive than large-group ones) or have a ratio of one observer to every
four talkers and have each observer clearly able to see and hear his four
speakers, when the discussion is set up.

☐ *EXERCISE*

*10 minutes' discussion and follow-up sessions – groups of four talkers and one
observer*

Speaker	Initiates statements	Argues against statements	Interrupts	Agrees simply	Questions to enlarge ideas	Enables another to speak
1						
2						
3						
4						

Mark each part of the conversation which fits these categories – they are
roughly in an assertive and then an enabling order: men often initiate, argue
and interrupt much more than women, who frequently take a passive or
enabling role. 'Enabling' includes all sorts of techniques that open up
discussions – e.g.
'You've had a lot of experience here ...'
'I noticed you didn't agree with that ...'
'You're looking a bit doubtful ...'

a) Discuss who initiates most statements and who argues against most
   statements?

Are these speakers male and do they help the discussion as well? (Somebody has to start it, so there's nothing wrong with being an initiator – it just depends how far and how often you push the discussion away from what the group wants.)

Breaking down barriers

b) Who are the main speakers who agree and do they also question and enable others?

Is there a pattern emerging in the group that some people already are quiet and unassertive? Ask them why they feel reluctant to contribute.

c) Remember that people who talk a lot may find this monitoring process offensive! People who talk very little may not want to discuss in front of the whole group why they are so quiet. Talking over the findings with people individually, or in small groups, can help them considerably to improve their confidence and discussion techniques.

5 Towards the next discussion

You may want to expand on these informal meetings into debates – there are full details about these in Chapter 10.

You may want to take a protest about a controversy further – have a look at Chapter 9: 'Protesting without violence'.

You may want to spend more time in small groups, deciding what is really worth discussing.

■ *EXERCISE*

The stick game (10 minutes for small groups, each with a stick + 5 minutes reporting back to large group)

a) Take a topic which will draw on everyone's experience – e.g.:

   1) What's the one subject that should be added to your present timetable?
   2) What's the ideal length of the school day?
   3) School holidays should never be longer than two weeks and neither should school terms.
   4) The school-leaving age is much too high.
   5) Nothing which is worth learning can be taught.

b) Write out your views and put them onto a stick, higher or lower to indicate their urgency.

c) The proposals that everyone puts highest must be the ones discussed first.

d) Report back to the larger group, if necessary with a minority report from the people who disagreed with what most people wanted.

For next time

You should have clear views about all these features – and how they affect *your* group (every group is different, so only you and the people in your group can decide what works best for you.)

1) What's the best layout of the room?
2) What's the best time limit?
3) How do we decide the wording of the topic?
4) Do we need a chairman?
5) What makes discussions go wrong? Individuals? Boring topics? People afraid to admit they're wrong? Failure to do anything with the decisions you've reached?
6) What makes a good discussion? Honesty? Readiness to listen? Anecdotes? Good leadership or none? Sharing ideas and worries?

2 Giving and receiving verbal instructions

This chapter concentrates on your giving and receiving information, explanations and instructions in a clear, direct way. There are a number of exercises which make you concentrate on speaking clearly and economically, and listening carefully and efficiently. This skill could get you a job, improve your memory or even save someone's life in an emergency.

STAGE 1 Face to face

1 Passing a message

Write down three sentences in which you leave messages for people you know: this could be telling them what's set for homework, what needs buying for dinner or what decorations and records you must bring to a Christmas party. Say the message to the next person in your group and then let the message be passed on within the group. As the other groups will be operating at the same time, you will have to be very clear about what your message is – shouting won't help: clear enunciation will.

When the last person has received the message, see if it is exactly what your first speaker intended. Then repeat the exercise with a different first speaker. Report back and see how successful you were in passing the message and where it went wrong – are some words harder to relay in a noisy classroom than others? Why?

2 Doctor's receptionist

Divide into groups of two, number yourself '1' and your partner '2'. Number 1 should be a very timid and quiet person, who has to give particulars of date of birth, name, reasons for wanting a doctor's appointment and the possible times, to Number 2, who should be a sensible, sympathetic receptionist. Number 1 should make Number 2's job as hard as possible, by whispering, mumbling and generally swallowing the information.

Then the situation should be reversed. Number 2 should play a very precise, clear-speaking patient dealing with a very impatient, slightly deaf receptionist, who will mis-hear and mis-spell as much information as possible. However much Number 2 is irritated by this, he or she should go on giving exact and clear information until an appointment is made. Afterwards, discuss what was hardest and easiest to understand.

3 Last ten pence at the phone box

Divide into groups of three. Number 1 has a broken-down car on a road that Number 2 also knows. Number 2 is the AA service centre, requiring exact information about the whereabouts of the car and what may be wrong with it. Number 3 is the telephone pips – he or she can decide how quickly the pips will sound, and must then time them exactly, warning Numbers 1 and 2 how long they are allowed. (The time should not exceed thirty seconds, which Number 3 can either count, silently, or time on a watch that the others don't see.)

After the pips, Numbers 1 and 2 are allowed ten seconds for final conversations before they are cut off.

Discuss after the exercise, whether there was enough clear information provided to send out a repair van with the right spare parts to the right place. Swap the roles, so that everyone has a chance to be victim, service centre and phone.

4 I'm lost

Give directions to the whole class for half a minute in answer to the enquiry – how do I get from *a* to *b*? You may decide the starting point and here are twenty-six places you can use:

Could you tell me the way to _____, please?

a) the nearest church; b) the police station; c) _____ supermarket; d) the public library; e) the Town (or Village) Hall; f) the art gallery; g) the museum; h) the nearest garage; i) the sports ground; j) the bus station; k) the railway station; l) the Job Centre; m) the Post Office; n) _____ restaurant; o) _____ football ground; p) _____ Bank; q) the hospital; r) the Primary School; s) _____ Comprehensive School; t) _____ industry; u) a newsagent; v) a baker; w) a chemist; x) a telephone; y) a doctor; z) a dentist.

Check for reception: Was the speaker: audible? clear? authoritative? informative? effective? Did every word contribute to the information? Did he/she use fillers (sort of; you know; I mean; 'em, 'er) or was the information direct and uncluttered?

5 What's on

Give an announcement of not more than half a minute which must contain: the event; the date; the time; the venue and information on booking. Choose one of the following:

a)	a play at a theatre	o)	a tennis tournament
b)	a film at a local or nearby town cinema	p)	a cricket match
		q)	a jumble sale
c)	a school concert	r)	a school second-hand clothing sale
d)	a school visit		
e)	a football match (or other game)	s)	a bring and buy for Save the Children
f)	a memorial service		
g)	a church social	t)	a caravan rally
h)	a youth club meeting	u)	a drama festival
i)	a protest meeting	v)	a sponsored walk
j)	a horeseshow event	w)	an orchestra rehearsal
k)	a motor race meeting	x)	a carol service
l)	a careers meeting	y)	a visit from local radio to the school
m)	an open day at school		
n)	a swimming gala	z)	a Hallowe'en party

Check reception: Did the announcement make you want to support the event? Did you remember all the essential details? Did everybody *listen*?

6 Half-minute sales

You have a personal possession which you are selling. Prepare a half-minute spot to give full details of the article; the price you want; when and where the transaction will be completed and your reason for selling it. Make sure that the details and the price are realistic; choose something that you know (even if you don't want to sell it!), e.g.:

a) bicycle
b) tennis racquet
c) cricket bat
d) guitar
e) record player
f) cassette recorder
g) transistor radio
h) computer game
i) camera
j) watch
k) books
l) sports gear
m) snooker table

n) dart board
o) tent
p) fishing rod
q) digital watch
r) school blazer
s) skis
t) electronic keyboard
u) video
v) typewriter
w) roller skates
x) calculator
y) slide projector
z) brief case

Check reception: Did you (the listeners) receive adequate information? Was it audible? Was it persuasive? Were the listeners attentive?

7 Two-minute boxing match

Now divide into groups of three. Number 1 will be the salesman or saleswoman, Number 2 will be the potential buyer and Number 3 will be the referee. Number 1 has half a minute to make a sales pitch, which must be scored by Number 3, who marks down a point for every punch which hits home – i.e. for every clear piece of information conveyed. At the end of this half-minute, Number 2, who has been listening carefully, takes up details with Number 1 and asks for more specific information – e.g. what sort of gears the bicycle has, whether there is any damage to the paintwork, why the price is so high, what guarantee the seller is giving. Number 1 must provide convincing answers to these questions – Number 3 will award a point for every answer that is well made and persuasive to the seller (Number 1) and a point for every objection which seems better argued to the buyer (Number 2).

At the end of two minutes, Number 3 should award the other two their points and explain why they were allotted. This will probably lead to further arguments which the teacher will finally umpire, preferably re-running the sales of the groups who appear to have scored the most points. The class can then listen to the best arguments and judge how they would award points.

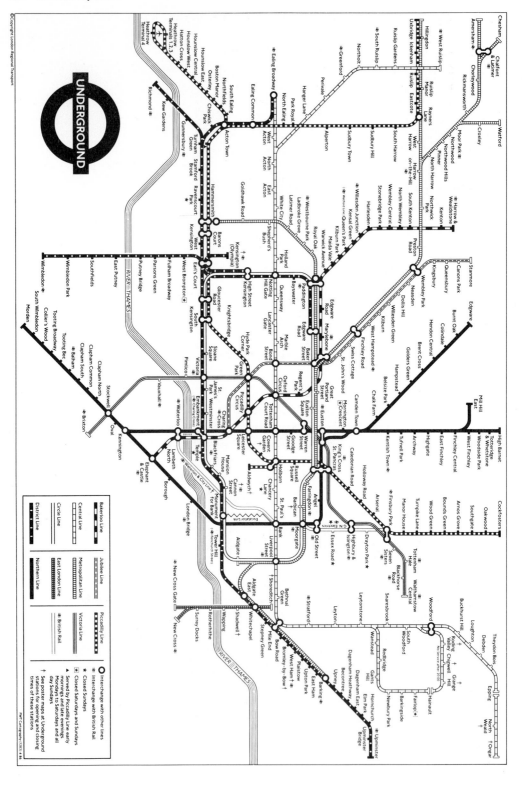

8 Giving detailed directions, using a map

On the opposite page is an Underground map of London. Each line has a different colour and at certain points, the lines meet and are marked with circles. These are the stations where you can change lines. As you will probably have to make a journey like the ones suggested below when you travel through London (for a holiday, a shopping expedition, a football match or a show), work out and memorise how you would make *one* of the journeys suggested (in each case, only one change of line is needed). If you have an overhead projector and a colour map of the London Underground, this would help communicate your instructions.

Example: *How do I get from Oxford Circus to Highgate?*
At Oxford Circus take the Central line to Tottenham Court Road. At Tottenham Court Road change to the Northern Line for the train to Highgate.

How do I get from:

1. Oxford Circus to Hammersmith?
2. Notting Hill Gate to Waterloo?
3. Baker Street to Covent Garden?
4. Golders Green to Oxford Circus?
5. Paddington to Finsbury Park?
6. Liverpool Street to Piccadilly Circus?
7. Charing Cross to Great Portland Street?
8. Arsenal to the Oval?
9. Leicester Square to Victoria?
10. Monument to Regents Park?
11. Hyde Park Corner to St Pauls?
12. Morden to Great Portland Street?
13. Richmond to Euston?
14. Cockfosters to Oxford Circus?
15. Wimbledon to Oxford Circus?
16. Finchley Road to Paddington?
17. Paddington to Finchley Road?

18 Kings Cross to Woodford?	25 Euston to Marble Arch?
19 Stanmore to St Pauls?	26 Oval to Kings Cross?
20 Uxbridge to Earls Court?	27 St Pauls to Barking?
21 Earls Court to Uxbridge?	28 Finsbury Park to Baker Street?
22 Covent Garden to Victoria?	29 Charing Cross to Wood Green?
23 Edgware to Marble Arch?	30 Euston to Kensington High
24 Elephant & Castle to Padd- ington?	Street?

Check reception:
1 Was the information given in a friendly manner?
2 Was the voice pleasant to listen to?
3 Was the instruction correct?
4 Were the names of places said clearly?
5 Was it said slowly enough to be remembered by the listener?
6 Was it clear enough to be understood by an overseas visitor?

9 Local tours

You may feel that you're not likely to need a working knowledge of the London Underground, so it would be more practical to test these skills on local areas. Some material may have to be provided by the teacher to help you do this, but, working in small groups, one guide and two or three listeners can quickly see whether a set of instructions is helpful and accurate. Keep within a one-minute time limit.

a) Using a street map of an area you know, give exact instructions to a French lorry-driver with a 38 ton juggernaut on how to reach the main road out of town from your house, where he has inadvertently arrived. Remember that you must take him through a route which is suitable for a large lorry, and give your instructions slowly and clearly. (Fluent French speakers may want to try this exercise in French.)

b) Using a local bus timetable, work out whether you can get back from any of the following using public transport:

1) a film that ends at 21.50 at a cinema 15 minutes away from the central bus station;
2) a careers evening at the nearest Technical College, which ends at 20.30;
3) a late night party which is unlikely to end before midnight.

Explain to the other members of the group which bus you would catch for each occasion, what time you would need to leave to catch the bus, and what time you would arrive home (add on time taken to walk from the nearest bus-stop to your home).

c) Using an Ordnance Survey map, work out the route of a 10–15 mile cycle race which would include as many hills as possible and keep away from main roads. Explain the route to the rest of the group, pointing out the best places for starting and finishing, with comments on any hazards.

d) Using a local tourist guide, work out the best order in which to walk or drive to the five most interesting local tourist attractions, and say how long this trip would take and why you've arranged it in this order. Detail the cost of making the round trip, if there are charges for admission or car parking costs.

e) Produce an anti-tourist trip, using your local knowledge and a street map. Work out and describe a route which would put off visitors and shock councillors into providing amenities in your local area. Again, try to include as many places in as short a route as possible.

10 Robots

Give exact instructions (preferably in pairs) for a very simple action – doing up a shoe, putting on a tie, dialling or tapping a number on a phone in the dark, opening a window. The person receiving the instructions must do only  what is said – assume nothing – you are being pro-grammed, and if the instructor forgets to tell you to move your feet, arms or body to the exact space required, don't help by doing this for him or her. Take all instructions literally and see how long it takes to perform actions that need precise descriptions, even though they are usually taken for granted.

☐ *GROUP EXERCISE*

Composing and delivering vital instructions

As briefly and clearly as you can, compose, in writing, instructions for the following emergencies and situations. Write independently then read your instructions to one another in your group. Each one will have weak points, each one valuable points. Create *one* complete instruction collectively taking the best points from each, then choose a spokesman to *read it aloud* when you join the whole group.

Group 1   Fire instructions for evacuating a school
Group 2   Fire instructions for evacuating hotel bedrooms

Group 3   Instructions for preventing and dealing with forest fires
Group 4   Warning instructions for high-voltage electricity cables
Group 5   Instructions for a coin-operated washing machine
Group 6   Instructions for using a lifebelt for a boating lake
Group 7   Warning instructions against drinking contaminated water
Group 8   Warning instructions for a deep-freeze cabinet in case of power cut
Group 9   Warning instructions to be printed on an electric blanket label
Group 10 Warning instructions on plastic bags

Class United: After ten minutes, break from your group and face the front where the speaker will stand. After the speaker from each group has read aloud – or better still – *spoken* the instructions, the class can judge the following points:

1 Could everyone in the class *hear*?
2 Was the instruction given slowly and clearly enough for it to be *remembered*?
3 Was it brief and to the point?
4 Were the instructions in logical order?
5 Could there be any confusion?

Listening test: If you have time, choose a person from each group to give *from memory* the instructions of another group. In this way 20 people will have spoken in front of the class and *all* will have spoken within groups.

---

11 Commercial instructions

Collect from home: labels, instructions and 'guarantees' and analyse the statements. Read your label aloud and invite comments based on the following questions where relevant:

1 Are the contents correctly described?
2 Are exaggerated claims being made?
3 Are some of the contents valueless or positively harmful?
4 Are some of the contents merely additives, preservatives or colourings?
5 Are the instructions logical and fool-proof?
6 *What* are the makers guaranteeing when they say, for example, 'Guaranteed for one year'?

Here are some words which may be of help to you in the criticism of the trades descriptions and the commentary:

Is it?
accurate, arresting, clear, concise, economical, explicit, honest, informative, instructive, logical, memorable, neat, practical, precise, reliable, simple.

Or is it?
inaccurate, boring, confused, uneconomical, muddled, evasive, cloudy, illogical, dull, untidy, impractical, vague, misleading, pretentious, exaggerated.

12 Persuasive speech in commercial selling

Choose six volunteers to 'sell' a product on commercial television. Remember that every second costs money so reduce your persuasive advertisement to 20 seconds or less.

Active listening and response

a) Did the speaker make you want to buy the product?
b) How did he do this?
   1) With tone of voice?
   2) Persuasive words?
   3) Catchy rhyme?

c) Was the face expressive and in keeping with the product and words?

d) How would you *resist* buying the product?
   1) Were the claims exaggerated?
   2) Inaccurate?
   3) Too vague?
   4) Deliberately misleading?

e) Did the speaker keep within the 20 seconds limit?

Remember that the public is being pressurized by every gimmick available. Trained actors are used to put the ideas across with every trick of photography, music and graphics to beguile the viewer. If you have a shot at doing this yourself you will not be so easily 'conned' when you are watching commercial television. (Has it occurred to you, for example, that the 'hole in the mint' is a simple way of doing you out of a quarter of the sweet? The packet is neatly filled with a third of holes!)

Here are some words which would suggest the variety of *tone* you might use depending on the product chosen:

a) alluringly
b) authoritatively
c) charmingly
d) concisely
e) confidently
f) crisply
g) distinctly
h) eagerly
i) enthusiastically
j) explicitly
k) expressively
l) graphically
m) heartily

n) humorously
o) imaginatively
p) logically
q) lucidly
r) memorably
s) persuasively
t) plainly
u) seductively
v) simply
w) sympathetically
x) tersely
y) unctuously
z) zanily

STAGE 2   You and the telephone

Remember that you can't be seen

The first important point to remember when you are telephoning is so obvious that it might not seem to be worth saying – but it is the key to all that follows. This means:

a) that you are not recognised and therefore you must introduce yourself, your firm or your school immediately;
b) that your face and smile are also not seen, so this warmth of tone and buoyant personality must come through your voice and the courtesy of your speech;
c) the body-language communication which we all use in the face-to-face situation with eyes, hands and facial muscles also cannot be seen; therefore words must be more precisely and directly used, and the 'sort of', 'kind of', 'you know', 'er' and 'em', 'I mean' fillers eliminated.

Time is short

Telephone time is expensive, also you do not know what activity or pressing engagement your call may be interrupting; so never go to the telephone either to make a call or receive one, without paper and pencil. You do not know who else may be wanting to use the line in either direction. It is therefore important to know what you want to say, and to say it with the brief courtesies which precede and conclude any normal conversation.

Memo pad

If you have information to give which includes names, times, dates, appointments, addresses, be sure that your *recipient* has pencil and paper and time to write the facts down. It is wise to *repeat* the items as a further check. Make a note yourself of any appointment and enter it in the appropriate day book or diary *at once*.

Telephoning out (you as the 'caller' in a call-box)

Read all the instructions given in the directories and code books carefully. You can save time and money by knowing correct codes and the various charge rates. Telephone sets and systems vary, so check that you have the appropriate coins and understand the relevant method and particular instrument. Remember that operator-controlled calls cost more.

Announcing your name

Give your full name: 'This is Jennifer Jones speaking', or Gerald Goodman etc. If it is a call to a shop where the speaker is not known, then the Mr Mrs or Miss is expected.

If you are speaking on behalf of your school, college or firm, announce the name clearly, slowly and pleasantly. If the call is on behalf of your employer, then explain your role, e.g. 'This is Mr Bloggs' secretary speaking, he has asked me to tell you ...' etc. Make sure that you are speaking to the person required or that the message is duly recorded and will be conveyed.

You as the 'receiver'

As soon as you lift the receiver, give either: (a) the telephone number; (b) the name of the firm; or (c) your own name, depending on the circumstances.

WARNING NOTE: If you are in the house alone, either in your own home, or as a baby-sitter in someone else's house, be guarded in your reply. Say the number only and wait until the caller has established his or identity before you reply. Don't say you are alone in the house to a stranger.

If you are an employee, announce the name of the firm clearly, followed by 'Can I help you?' If the call is for your employer or another department, answer with one of the following alternatives, altering the details to suit the particular case:

a) 'This is Mr Bloggs' secretary speaking. I am so sorry Mr Bloggs is out at a meeting (*or whatever reason is appropriate*). May I take a message?'
b) 'Will you hold the line a moment, please, and I will see if Mr Bloggs is available?'

YTS students at Solihull

c) 'If you will hold the line I'll put you through to his office ... You're through now.'
d) 'Mr Bloggs will be sorry to have missed you. Shall I ask him to call you back?' (*Check on name, number and suitable time.*)
e) 'Yes, I'll put you through to the soft furnishing department ... Mr Jones is on the line now.'

f)   'Good afternoon, Mr Harrison. Mr Bloggs asked me to tell you, if you rang, that the goods have arrived and that he is most grateful for the way you've put this order through so quickly.'

General points

Much confusion can be caused by vague or inaccurate passing on of messages. Therefore:

1) Keep a pencil and pad by the telephone.
2) If in *any doubt*, spell out aloud the name and address of the person giving the message or the person who is concerned with the message.
3) Repeat all numbers, prices, times and dates, and write them down.
4) If it is an invitation of a fairly formal nature, make sure that your reply fully confirms and thanks the caller or gives a courteous explanation of why you can't accept.
5) If a call-back is necessary, check with the caller about the times he or she will be available.

■ *EXERCISE*

Telephone role-playing

Choose a partner and work in pairs on any *one* of the following situations. Two telephones should be provided for the class. It may not be possible to have actual telephones for every pair working separately and simultaneously, in that case, the telephone must be simulated. Rehearse in pairs on one of the exercises allotted to you.

Decide which one shall be the caller and which the receiver. Put your chairs back to back so that you cannot communicate visually. Make sure that you each have a pad and pencil, and check afterwards that the essential facts, correctly spelt, have been recorded.

1) Your dog is ill. Telephone the veterinary surgeon.
2) Telephone the police to report a motor accident.
3) Ring up a garage to ask for help for a car which has broken down.
4) You are baby-sitting and the baby is not well. Telephone the baby's mother.
5) You are inviting a local councillor to visit your group and, having already sent a letter, you are checking on times, room, etc. and giving a final welcome.

6) FIRE
7) AMBULANCE
8) POLICE

In each case give a clear location and brief description of the fire, accident or disturbance.

9) Telephone the gas company about a leaking pipe.
10) Telephone the water board for a similar emergency.
11) Your TV set is out of order. Telephone to ask for someone to come and repair it.
12) Telephone to book seats for a certain performance at a theatre
13) Telephone on behalf of a firm (think out a specific one) to the Job Centre about a vacant situation.
14) A carpet has been bought and delivered. Telephone to arrange for a fitter to come to complete the work.
15) Telephone the post-office on behalf of an old lady who is moving to a rest home and give the change of address.

Exercises 1–15 were formal and brief and did not require anything more than facts, figures and politeness.

Exercises 16–29 are more demanding on the social skills of tact, courtesy, persuasion, appreciation etc.

Again in pairs, choose *one* of the following:

16) You are planning a coffee morning or bring & buy sale. Telephone someone you know *slightly*, asking if he or she will co-operate, and if so in what way.
17) Your school (club, church) are doing jobs for charity. Telephone an adult friend of your parents explaining the project and asking if you can offer your services. In the most tactful and polite way you can make it clear that, in this case, it has to be paid for!
18) You have found a stray cat; ring up the police and report it. (If it is not claimed you could later ring the RSPCA or pet shop or a private person to arrange about adoption.)
19) Your mother has been taken ill that morning and you are staying at home to look after her. Telephone the school, explaining the reason for your absence.
20) You are captain of a team and are ringing up another school (club, team, college, works) to arrange a fixture.
21) You are leader of a pop group; telephone a local hostess about arrangements for playing at a dance she is organising.
22) You have been shopping and have left a parcel in one of the shops. Telephone your enquiry about its loss.
23) You have been interviewed for a job and have been accepted. You afterwards remember that you did not say that your summer holidays had already been booked for certain dates. Ask politely by telephone if this arrangement can still be accepted.
24) You have been invited to be either a bridesmaid or, if a boy, a best man or an usher at your friend's wedding. Ring up to get to know more details and accept or refuse according to your own situation.

25) Your aunt (uncle, grandparents . . .) have invited you to spend part of the holidays with them. Answer the invitation, getting to know details of dates, times and travel.

26) You are offering to help on Saturday mornings at a pre-school play-group (or old people's home, blind home, hospital, farm, etc.). Ask in what way you can be helpful, and arrange times, etc. Make it clear if there are any days when you cannot be there.

27) Your class is going by coach to visit a factory (ancient buildings, museum, art gallery . . .). Book the coach by telephone, giving all details of place, date, times, numbers. (This should be confirmed by letter.)

28) Four of you are hiring a boat to sail on a canal. Make enquiries about cost, equipment, fuel, place of departure, etc.

29) Make a long-distance call to your home (or, if you are not on the telephone, to friends who will give the message) after you have had a long, difficult journey. Do not reverse the charge, and keep within three minutes.

Class evaluation check on two or three pairs selected for a repeat performance using the hand set

1) Were the names of caller and called clearly said and, if necessary, spelt?
2) Did the speakers sound friendly and courteous?
3) Was the information helpful, direct and complete?
4) Was it fully explanatory?
5) When it was necessary, were the speakers tactful, persuasive or business-like?
6) Was *time* used efficiently?

CHAPTER

3 Communicating skills

1 Who's influenced you?

Most skills (including speech) are acquired from imitation – you watch, listen and learn.

Learning from one another

■ *EXERCISE*

5 minutes maximum – work in pairs

a) Make a list of any skills you'd claim to have: include everything – from Cub and Brownie badges to Saturday jobs to basic abilities – getting on with people, writing, singing, swimming, riding a bicycle, etc.

b) Tell your partner how you came to have these skills. If you can remember the stages in which you acquired a more recent one (e.g. skiing, playing an instrument, writing computer programs), outline these; say what problems you had at each stage and how you overcame them.

c) Change round. Hear your partner's list and discuss who helped to build these skills.

d) Report back to the group and decide how far any of these qualities in your teacher helped you:
enthusiasm, expert knowledge, patience, varied methods, sense of humour, personal awareness of your needs, forceful delivery, readiness to let you make mistakes.

---

2 Choose your own skill – an individual project

Here are a number of suggestions:

a) Choose one of these that you know well and can talk about in an interested way for a couple of minutes:

1 Wiring an electric plug 2 Mending a fuse 3 Rewiring a room	or any other job that involves the use of electricity
4 Projecting a transparency 5 Developing a film	or any other skill connected with filming or recording
6 Preparing a fishing line 7 Basic moves in chess 8 Taking a brass rubbing	or any other aspect of sport or hobbies demanding a manual or mental skill
9 Navigating a boat 10 Controlling sails	or any other aspect of yachting or sailing
11 Cutting out a dress pattern	or any sewing or embroidery skill
12 Making an omelette 13 Making a souffle	or any other cookery technique

Asking the right questions and learning from the skilled adult

14 Using a freezer
15 Using a washing machine
16 Changing a tyre
17 Changing car plugs   or any other domestic or
18 Wine-making   gardening skill
19 Rose pruning
20 Taking plant cuttings

21 Driving a combine harvester
22 Using a milking machine
23 Grooming a horse
24 Dove-tailing wood   or the use of any other tools
25 Welding metals
26 Using an electric drill

27 Setting hair   or any other hairdressing process

28 Use and care of paintbrushes   or 'do-it-yourself' technique

29 Pitching a tent   or camping or hiking skill

30 A chemistry experiment   or biology, physics

31 A mathematical demonstration	or archaeology, astronomy, geography
32 Use of a cash register or a computer	or other measuring device
33 Basic rules in ski-ing 34 Swimming strokes 35 Ballet positions	or other artistic or athletic technique
36 Crochet, knitting or weaving processes	or other handicraft
37 Stringing a guitar	or the care of any other musical instrument

A kidney patient explaining the operation and treatment

38 Using the STD dialling system 39 Telephoning a telegram or telex message	or other operation connected with the telephone system
40 Defrosting a refrigerator 41 Using coin-operated launderette 42 Changing a typewriter ribbon 43 Using a photocopier 44 Using a compass 45 Using a kitchen blender 46 Using an electric sewing machine 47 Making a microscopic slide	or the care, use or maintenance of any gadgets or equipment

48 Surfing – or other water skills ⎫
49 Correct use of lanes on a motorway ⎬ or use of the highway code
50 Reading an ordnance map ⎭   or driving techniques

51 Packing and registering a parcel   or any other Post Office activity

52 Cutting a stencil for duplicating   or other office processes

53 Flag signalling in motor racing   or the use of other
                                                       signalling devices

54 Recording rainfall   or other meteorological skill

55 Checking a pulse rate   or other nursing activities

56 Using a thermostat   or other aspects of heat control
                                                       and dispersal

57 Tie-dying   or other decorative crafts

b) Make a clear running order of points, which you can summarise on a piece of paper and refer to, if you lose your way. If there are five points, make sure that each is given the right length of time (e.g. 20 seconds each in a two-minute talk, giving you time to sum up at the end).

c) Add diagrams or props which will make the talk more interesting. Arrange these in the right order so they are ready to use and also remind you of the order in which you will be describing the process.

d) Try a practice run, with a friend to time you and comment on what you said. If you are going to speak in a large room try and find a similar one to practise in. Your friend should sit as far away as possible and tell you if you go too fast or speak too softly. Also, your diagrams and props may benefit from being a bit larger or displayed in a different way.

Here is a simple process clearly illustrated: this could form the basis of a two-minute talk:

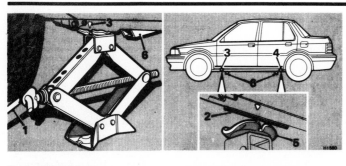

Road wheel changing
WARNING: The vehicle jack is designed for wheel changing only. Ensure that the surface on which the base of the jack is to bear is firm, level and free of loose material.
Apply the handbrake, select 1st gear manual gearbox or '**P**' automatic gearbox and place chocks at the front and rear of the wheel diagonally opposite to the one to be removed.

Fit the handle (1) to the jack, rotate it clockwise to extend the jack and position it under the reinforced area of the body flange (2) nearest the wheel to be removed. Use the flange (3) for the front wheels and flange (4) for the rear wheels. Ensure that the jack head (5) is positioned under the reinforced jacking point as illustrated.

CAUTION: Do not use the tubular bar section (6) adjacent to the side reinforced jacking areas for lifting or support.

Extend the jack to take the weight of the car, and remove the hub cover using the tool provided. Slacken the wheel nuts by turning them half a turn anti-clockwise. Raise the car until the tyre is clear of the ground, remove the wheel nuts and lift off the wheel.

Ensure the wheel locating spigot is clean and lightly oiled. Place the spare wheel on the studs and locate the spigot, fit the wheel nuts with their tapered ends towards the wheel and lightly tighten.
Lower the car and remove the jack and wheel chock, tighten the wheel nuts in diagonal sequence. Check and adjust tyre pressures.

Refit the hub cover.
As soon as possible have the tyre pressure and the tightness of the road wheel nuts checked.

Have the wheel balanced and the tyre of the spare wheel repaired or replaced.

Stowing the spare wheel
Fit the strap to the road wheel and lift the wheel into the luggage compartment and retain in position with the screw clamp. Position the jack, jack handle, wheel nut spanner and wheel trim in the plastic moulding. Refit the luggage compartment floor covering.

3 Personal checkpoint

When you have given your talk, check the following points

a) Did I look at my listeners in a friendly way?
b) Did I handle my props so that everyone could see them?
c) Did I pause to make eye-contact with my listeners?
d) Did I say what I wanted to in a clear and animated way?
e) Did I use fillers: 'sort of', 'like', 'you know', 'I mean', '...er...' '...em...', 'or something'?
    (It is a good idea to *pause*, to take a deep breath, then when your new thought is ready – speak! It won't keep your listeners waiting long but it will give them time to 'receive'.)
f) Were the words I used appropriate and interesting?
g) Did I make the most of my time?

4 The examiner's view

When you have heard another person's talk, put yourself in the place of an oral examiner.

□ *EXERCISE*

15 minutes – 1 speaker and 2 or 3 examiners in each group

a) Listen to a two-minute talk.

b) Fill in this chart, as fairly and generously as you can. There are no absolute answers, but it will help the speaker know what impact a talk has made. If you think a speaker knows exactly what he or she is doing and is skilful in handling materials, this would be shown by a tick in Box 5 on the top line. The speaker's speech, voice and manner can be judged in the same way on the lower lines. Finally give an honest view of how much *you* have learnt – just a vague impression (worth 1 or 2) or an exact knowledge of how to reproduce the process the speaker described (5).

Name	*Skill*				
	1	*2*	*3*	*4*	*5*
Skill with gear					
Skill with words					
Agreeable to listen to					
Confident and relaxed manner					
Audience have precise idea of how to practise this skill					

c) Discuss your scores with the other examiners and the speaker.

STAGE 2   You as an investigator

Two minutes hardly does justice to most people's jobs which take many years to learn completely. The exercises below suggest ways of giving longer talks on skills and work.

1 A day in the life

If you are trying to give an impression of a daily routine, it is easy, but misleading, to highlight the memorable moments. A more accurate picture will emerge if you fill in a timetable and add up the different amounts of time spent working hard, working a little and doing anything but work. Use the timetable grid below to work out what you do with your week – add up the total amount of

a) leisure activities
b) work
c) sleep
d) functions (eating, washing, etc.)
e) doing nothing.

■ *EXERCISE*

15 minutes + follow-up discussion – work individually, then in pairs

a) Copy out this timetable for all your time in an average school/college week.

	Monday	Tuesday	Wednesday	Thursday	Friday	Saturday	Sunday
Midnight							
1 a.m.							
2 a.m.							
3 a.m.							
4 a.m.							
5 a.m.							
6 a.m.							
7 a.m.							
8 a.m.							
9 a.m.							
10 a.m.							
11 a.m.							
Midday							
1 p.m.							
2 p.m.							
3 p.m.							
4 p.m.							
5 p.m.							
6 p.m.							
7 p.m.							
8 p.m.							
9 p.m.							
10 p.m.							
11 p.m.							

b) Now add up the amount of time you spend on the five categories – leisure activities, work, sleep, functions and doing nothing. (Whether you include passive pastimes like watching TV or sitting listening to records as 'activities' or 'doing nothing' is worth discussing with the group.) The total should be 268 hours, but a rough estimate will do!

c) Compare your results with your partner's and say which totals surprise you and why.

d) How much of your week does represent some form of skill? Should more be spent on different activities?

---

2 Other people's lives

If you are going to give an impression of somebody else's day, your talk could use the timetable structure; you won't need to account for every one of 24 hours, but a clear sequence will help the audience follow what you're describing and relate it to their own experience.

■ *EXERCISE*

Project in student's own time

a) Interview one of the people who has influenced you (see page 4). See Chapter 5 for advice on interviews, if you are not sure where to start.

b) Prepare a detailed list of questions before you speak to the person. If you have a cassette to record the conversation in full, this will be very useful to work from later.

c) Take from this account a clear set of headings around which to build your talk, e.g. best and worst moments, morning and afternoon, going to work and leaving, money or job satisfaction? Training, experience and common sense – what does the job need most?

d) As with your two-minute talk, divide what you have to say into clear and balanced sections. Time and rehearse your talk first with a friendly but critical partner.

3 Communicating other people's skills

The passage below from Ronald Blythe's *Akenfield* is spoken by a Suffolk orchard-owner. (Wages refer to 1960s' rates.)

■ *EXERCISE*

30 minutes + follow-up discussion – work individually, then in pairs

Assume you can only include half the material in your talk. To convey the man's work and feelings, which sections would you:

a) summarise?

b) omit?

c) quote directly?

1

The year begins after the picking. We start pruning. We look at the trees and say, 'This is the fruit bud, this is the leaf bud', and we wonder at the prospect of good blossom. Except with pears, for you can never tell with pears. A heavy blossom show never means a heavy crop. It seems to me that the pears thin themselves out. You'll get a pear orchard covered in bloom and worth anybody's time to walk down, the trees will all 'set' and then, just as you expect them to bulb-up, half of the fruit buds will drop off. It is the tree sorting itself out. Unlike the Bramley – they won't drop off and during a great blossom year like that of 1965, we had to go round with ladders and thin them by hand. It was a terrible job. You'd find a cluster of blossoms with seven or eight apples in a heap and you have to take three or four out and throw them to the ground in mid-June. Because, always in June you get what we call the 'June drop', when plum-sized apples will drop to the grass automatically. But now we have a spray which does the thinning-out. The Coxes were sprayed by an aeroplane this year. It was done three or four days before they were picked to prevent store-rot.

2

During the picking season, you'll get twenty to twenty-five young people coming to the orchards for a job. Most of them stop about a couple of days – they don't like ladder work! They come with visions of a lovely holiday, sunbathing, transistors, larking about and a pound or two right easy at the end of each day. But they can't use the ladders. They will lay it flat, like a thatcher on a stack, and break the trees with their weight. The straighter a ladder is put up, the better. I put the ladder up for them and show them how to pick. Just turn the apple up, put it gently into the pail and when the pail is full, empty it softly into the box below by letting the apples fall across your arm.

3

They'll do this for about half an hour, then they'll think that they're not getting along nearly fast enough, and you'll hear the apples rattling down into the orchard! They'll be throwing them in the pail. The picking of the tree-fruit is really controlled by nine special women – our regulars, we call them. These nine will pick eighty acres of fruit, earning between £10–£12 a week. They come to the orchards at various times after they have managed to get their housework done, mostly between 8.30 and 4.30 and they only stop for a flask of tea. In the old days, when people were hard up, the orchards were crowded with women at picking time. Nowadays, the women work in twos and threes, one picking from the ground, one collecting the middle apples and one picking from the top of the ladder. Each orchard is planted in six or eight rows and the women strip it row by row. It doesn't matter how tall a tree is, there is never a single apple left on it. Although they pick fast, their hands are so gentle that you never find a bruised apple. It is a miracle.

4

The children come for work as soon as they have broken up for their summer holiday at the end of July. Those who are in their last year at school are often hoping for a regular job. The boys and girls are good on the gooseberries and currants. Top pickers on gooseberries can earn as much as £5 a day. The currant fields are being extended all the time and we now have thirty-six acres of them altogether. About half of these currants are being picked in a new drastic fashion, with the entire bush being cut off close to the ground and fed into a picker made out of a converted hop machine. It is an experiment which, I think, came from Kent. The bushes can be grown very close together and you can get twice as many on the same acreage. The only snag which we have come up against is that the bushes don't grow enough the second year to warrant their being cropped down again. It is a strange sort of picking. There is this great field covered with thick bushes one day, and as bare as a bit of ploughing the next.

d) Make notes on your talk.

e) Fill out your notes in a talk to your partner and see whether he or she feels you've conveyed the spirit of the original.

A list of other accounts of work is given in the bibliography at the end of this book; you should find a number of personal and entertaining descriptions there, which can be adapted for talks.

---

4 Teachers are human

The one person immediately available in any school or college who has a job, an interest in you and long experience of talking is . . . your teacher.

■ *EXERCISE*

As long as your teacher allows – in groups of two or three

a) Below is an account by a sixth-form teacher about her typical day. Read it through.

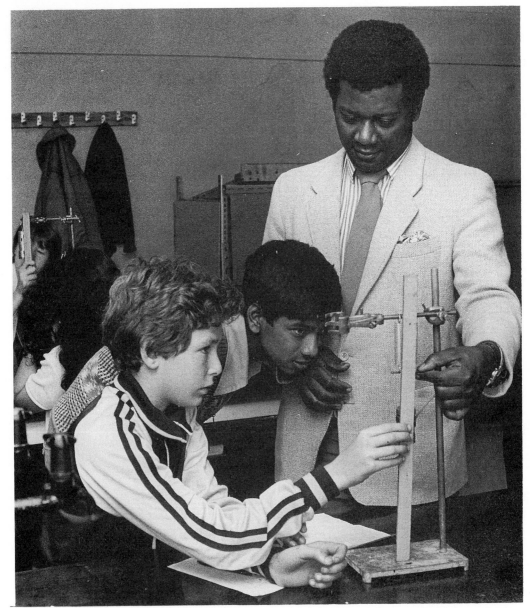

Precision and concentration in communicating measuring skills

b) Next, discuss and write down all the questions that would produce a similar, true and entertaining account of your teacher's skills and stresses.

c) Compare the questions you have produced with another group's. Agree on five which incorporate everybody's best ideas.

d) Arrange with your teacher to answer these questions, either in front of the whole group or in a private interview.

(This is a useful and immediate check on the ways reporters can distort a person's comments and intentions: there are more detailed examinations of reporting in Chapter 10.)

LONG DAY'S JOURNEY INTO NIGHT: *or*, A DAY IN THE LIFE OF A DT (Divisional Tutor)

7:15 a.m. Gloom and sleet herald the first day of Spring . . .

8:20 a.m. Attempt to shepherd children out of the house in organised fashion (husband already having zoomed off efficiently into the far distance). Daughter's lunch box falls open: cheese sandwiches all over patio. Dog eats one. Son treads on another, then remembers he needs his football boots. Doesn't know where they are. I don't either. Frenzied search.

8:35 a.m. Out onto Southport Road. Clench hands around steering wheel – just time to get to College promptly. Stare, horrified, as large tractor bearing mountainous load of carrots trundles out in front of me and proceeds ponderously on its way, shedding the odd vegetable onto the car bonnet. Rustics sitting on the back grin amiably at me.

8:42 a.m. Seems an eternity later. Tractor turns off into field, rustics waving cheerily. Speed along . . . and meet the back of another traffic jam. This one is behind a hearse. Is it possible to begin the day again, with a clean sheet?

8:52 a.m. Hurtle into College to take register. Tutor group have everything under control, and smile kindly at me. Colleague looks in to tell me that I've left the car lights on.

9:00 a.m. Lesson goes smoothly! Are things taking a turn for the better?

9:50 a.m. Optimism obviously seriously premature. Second years suffering badly from exam nerves: show a disconcerting tendency to write down everything I say. Immediately wish I were more capable of witty, articulate and penetrating comment. Wonder if they wrote down 'Good morning' when I said that.

10:40 a.m. Break. Deal with two students waiting outside door to consult me: feel even more strongly that I need to be Wisdom Personified. Arrive, late, at SCR to discover that tea-urn has failed to boil. Drink revolting cup of luke-warm coffee with little bits floating in it. Collapse briefly into chair by friends. Exchange wan smiles.

11:00 a.m. 'Free' period. Ha! Speak, successively, to three students who present various excuses for non-appearance at Recreational Activities, one of them of a stunning originality. Think of asking this student to take my next lesson. They go off (hopefully) to mend their wicked ways. I take out a set of essays, and . . .

11:50 a.m. . . . begin next period having corrected half a page, three more students having called in to ask for help with essays. Am profoundly glad they care, but wish someone had the job of helping me with my marking . . .

12:40 a.m. Lunch-time. Have salad in dining hall, trying not to drool over chips being consumed by others. Feel hungry, and buy a huge slab of shortbread (the biggest on the plate) on my way out. Coffee in SCR. At least it's hot this time. Discover, lurking in pigeonhole, three sets of Divisional reports, given in early. Is EVERYONE more on top of things than I am?? See a sinister gleam of yellow slips in two sets of them. No wonder they look fat.

2:00 p.m. Set essay for first year group, who immediately protest loudly that it's too difficult, they have fourteen other essays to do for Tuesday, the dog has rabies, etc. etc. Calm them down. We work out a sane and reasoned approach to the whole thing; now all they've got to do is get it written. Wonder whether Shakespeare would have managed? He only wrote the play.

3:00 p.m. Last lesson. Students claim exhaustion. They look very fresh from my side of the eyeballs: do they know what it's like this side? Animated discussion of the value of literature ensues. Wonder, not for the first time, why 'A' level examiners don't come down to the chalkface.

3:50 p.m. End of College day. Look at mountain of files, essays, texts, banda'd sheets, sticks of chalk on my desk, and wonder feebly what to do with them. Finally stuff them all into briefcase to take home. Briefcase refuses to shut. Contemplate bringing shopping trolley tomorrow.

4:15 p.m. Stagger to car. Put key into ignition, and turn. Not much happens. Try again. Think, for 999th time, that car maintenance classes would be a good idea. Stomp back into College full of self-pity. Caretakers cluster – very helpfully – round car. Eventually, with a very bad grace, it goes.

8:30 p.m. Family and dog fed: children in bed (more or less). Open briefcase. Tell myself to keep calm. Two sets of essays to mark, three sets of reports to read through. I love this job . . . that's why I do it . . . and tomorrow is another day . . .

V. R. Chadwick

5　Dramatise the day

■ *EXERCISE*

30 minutes – groups of three or four

Using this extract from Stud Terkel's *Working*, prepare a dramatic reading.

a) One person in the group is the gas-meter reader. One person is the listener. One person plays the people the speaker meets (e.g. the woman in section 2 and, if you're feeling resourceful, the German shepherd in section 1 (i.e. a large, fierce Alsatian dog). One person is the director (though he or she could also be the listener).

b) Work out a dramatic reading of this long passage; agree where to become more angry, more amused; where to speed up, where to slow down; where to move, stand still. (Alternatively, three members of the group could prepare a straight reading of the same parts of the extract: then each person reads and the others comment on the emphasis and how it differs from their interpretation and why).

1 I've been bit once already by a German shepherd. And that was something. It really was scary. It was an outside meter the woman had. I read the gas meter and was walking back out and heard a woman yell. I turned around and this German shepherd was comin' at me. The first thing I thought of was that he might go for my throat, like the movies. So I sort of crouched down and gave him my arm instead of my neck. He grabbed a hold of my arm, bit that, turned around. My arm was kinda soft, so I thought I'd give him something harder. So I gave him my hand. A little more bone in that. So he bit my hand.
I gave it to him so he wouldn't bite my throat. I didn't want him to grab hold of my face. He turned around again and by that time – they usually give you a three-cell flashlight, a pretty big one – I had that out and caught him right in the mouth. And he took the flashlight away from me. I jumped a six-foot fence tryin' to get away from him, 'cause then I had my senses back. It was maybe in five seconds this all happened.

Listener Were you badly hurt?

2 No. Just a hole right here in my arm. (*Indicates a livid scar.*) I was cussin' pretty good, too. She was tryin' to call the dog back, which made me turn around. Otherwise he'd probably got me in the back. I'm just glad I turned around.

You can usually tell if a dog's gonna bite ya. You're just waitin' for him to do somthin' and then you can clobber him. The gas company'll stay behind you in that sort of thing. That's the biggest part of a dog's day, when the gas man comes. (*Laughs.*)

I've gone into houses where the woman will say, 'Let me grab the dog. I don't want you to give him a hard time'. I've had one house where I was trying to make friends with the dog. He was a schnauzer. I started to walk away because it was just barking its little fool head off. It just fell over on its side. I thought it had a heart attack. She said, 'He usually relapses from barking too much.' She gave me a glare like it was my fault. Usually they'll say, 'Don't hit the dog.' If it's bad enough, I usually hit him in the head with the flashlight, to knock it away. Then they'll say, 'Why did you hit it? The dog's not gonna bite you'. I say, 'It's jumping on me, it's scratching me'. And she says, 'All it's doing is scratching you?' It's weird. It's not biting me, it's scratching me. (*Laughs.*) So that's okay.

Listener When nobody's looking . . . ?

3 You kick him down the stairs usually. (*Laughs.*) Usually the dog will follow you down the stairs or back up. That'll give you a good chance, 'cause the dog'll try to pass you. So you would kick him down the stairs. (*Laughs.*) Even if he just follows you down the stairs you try to get him for the one you missed a couple of houses back. Many people will report you if you abuse a dog. But what about me?

People complain to the company for jumping over their fences or going across their grass. I usually don't jump fences any more unless I'm in a hurry. The boss is usually nice about it. It'll get to him and he'll say, 'Okay, it won't happen again'. They mark down a code nine in the book: Do not cross the lawn or do not jump the fence. Older people that take care of their lawns don't like nobody to cross their lawns – which is kind of weird.

I got a good letter one time, not that I've gotten bad ones. I really deserve maybe six to ten letters. Maybe a woman was crippled in the house and I'll waste five, ten minutes of my time, and I'll say, 'I'll give you a cup of coffee'. And they'll say, 'Thanks a lot', and I'm on my way. What would it hurt to write in and say this guy really helped me out?

4 They don't want to be bothered to come to the door. They'd rather have something else to do than answer the doorbell and let the gas man in. Why can't they say, 'I don't want to admit you in my home at the present time cause it's dirty?' I can tell you something. Most of the houses are dirty, they're filthy. They stink. I have one woman, she's got fifteen cats and she's got 'em down in the basement. I'll walk down there and walk right out without reading the gas meter. Yeah, white middle class. Even in Wilmette, high class. The outside of the house is kept nice, beautiful, but when you get inside, when you get into the heart of it, it's filthy.

One guy was reading gas meters for eight years. He went to buy furniture. The next day he was supposed to read the gas meter at the store. He wanted me to go in because he didn't want the salesman to see him, to know that he was a gas meter reader. He was embarrassed. It doesn't really matter what kind of job you do, as long as you're working.

The meter readers is the bread of the whole company. Without these people being billed and having the money come into the gas company, the other employees wouldn't get paid. You have to know how to read a meter, 'cause if you make a mistake, it could be maybe the guy would pay another hundred dollars more. It's kinda tricky. There's four dials. The company gives you a high and a low. Let's say 3000 for the low and 5000 for the high. It's usually about 4000, right dead in the middle. You have to go there and make sure they're using the middle. I can read a meter from twenty-thirty feet away.

There are more suggestions on reading aloud in Chapter 6 and a detailed look at dialogue in action in Chapter 8.

STAGE 3   You as an assessor

You should, by now, have enough information to discuss the general issues below.

1 What's it worth?

☐ *EXERCISE*

A full lesson – groups of three or four

a) Decide what you think about these questions: one person in each group should make notes about the main viewpoints but everybody should be ready to report back briefly to the larger group at the end of 10–15 minutes' discussion:

Group 1: Which work has given you the most satisfaction? Why?
Did you have to make a great effort?
How did you feel about the result of your work?

Group 2: How would you spend an enjoyable day without spending money? (Assume that there is no TV, radio or telephone, but that basic food is available.)

What are they worth?

Group 3: Does society value people with manual skills as much as people with mental skills? Should it? How do we make people feel valued?

Group 4: As people have more and more free time, through early retirement, increasing technology, long periods of unemployment, how can they use their time constructively? Is it possible to teach people to use their leisure? What is done locally and what more could be done?

Group 5: Consider this list of average weekly wages paid to different occupations – are they fair?

£80 – waitress	£200 – junior advertising
£150 – head chef	executive
£300 – TV reporter on regional news	£250 – probation officer
£500 – First division footballer	£400 – short-haul air pilot
£700 – Best-selling author	£600 – Radio 1 disc jockey
£1000 – Prime Minister	£800 – Judge
	£2000 – Director of the
	National Coal Board

(all figures approximate and before tax, in 1985)

b) Report back to larger group and decide on a revised pay scale, with reasons.

---

2 Sum up your skills

The attached questions have been produced by a travel firm so that anyone applying to join them can have a comprehensive reference.

◼ *EXERCISE*

Full lesson – groups of two who know each other well

a) Fill in the form on page 53 for yourself; have your partner fill in the form for you.

b) Compare the results and decide why there are differences and which are the best features for a person working in a travel firm.

◼ *ALTERNATIVE EXERCISE*

Groups of two who don't know each other well

a) Agree on a job which you both know something about.

b) Compile a list of questions, similar to the travel firm's, which would bring out the skills and qualities the job would need.

NAME OF APPLICANT: ....

DATE EMPLOYED: ....

DATE OF TERMINATION: ....

POSITION HELD: ....

DID HE/SHE HAVE ANY PERSONAL PROBLEMS ....
THAT INTERFERED WITH THE JOB:

What was his/her working relationship with other members of staff?
☐EXCELLENT ☐GOOD ☐SATISFACTORY ☐POOR
Adaptability?
☐LEARNS QUICKLY ☐TEACHABLE ☐SLOW TO LEARN
Confidence?
☐INSPIRES OTHERS ☐NEEDS ENCOURAGEMENT ☐INDIFFERENT
Attendance & Punctuality?
☐EXCELLENT ☐GOOD ☐SATISFACTORY ☐POOR
How would you rate the quality of work performed?
☐EXCELLENT ☐GOOD ☐SATISFACTORY ☐POOR
How does he/she communicate?
a) Face to face...
☐GENIALLY ☐HELPFULLY ☐SHYLY ☐AWKWARDLY
b) On the telephone...
☐CLEARLY ☐CONSTRUCTIVELY ☐HALTINGLY ☐ABRUPTLY
Did you find this person to be honest and trustworthy?
☐YES/NO
Would you re-employ?
☐YES/NO
Individual's strong points and/or limitations?
_____

Was he/she required to handle money?
_____

Overall evaluation:
☐EXCELLENT ☐GOOD ☐SATISFACTORY ☐SOME DOUBTS ☐POOR

ADDITIONAL COMMENTS:

Signature: ....

Position: .... Date: ....

4 Discovering your voice

There are attractive and unattractive voices all over the world; they have nothing to do with region or money or class. If you mumble, through embarrassment; put an edge to your voice, through tension; talk too much, through not considering your listener, your voice immediately makes other people tense and communication becomes much more difficult.

So, the only way that you can be sure that your voice is going to be positive and worth listening to, is to use it clearly and confidently – don't adopt a 'hypercorrected' accent or mimic other people; be interested in what you're saying and your voice will be interesting in response. If you feel bored, your voice will be boring, too.

STAGE 1   Your voice

1   Try this exercise: walk round the room and greet every other member of the group you meet with 'Hello, how are you',

a) as if you really wanted to know and you were delighted to see the person.
b) as if you wished you could avoid this person more than anyone in the world and could barely say the sentence.

In (a) you should find that the way you speak, walk and move your hands and face differs completely from (b). Discuss how.

2   When you are talking to friends and feel relaxed, your voice has a wide range of notes; it moves from high notes to low notes effortlessly, it has an interesting variety of tones and it uses breath efficiently and smoothly.

3   When you are in pain or in a difficult situation (e.g. answering questions reluctantly, losing your temper, feeling guilty), your voice will be limited to middle notes with flat tones.

This is because you feel that the questioner is interested in the mere factual answer, rather than in you yourself. Consequently, you tend to hold yourself back, keeping your jaw tight and your teeth closed, and you mumble. Perhaps

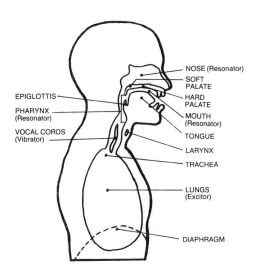

NOSE (Resonator)
SOFT PALATE
EPIGLOTTIS
HARD PALATE
PHARYNX (Resonator)
MOUTH (Resonator)
VOCAL CORDS (Vibrator)
TONGUE
LARYNX
TRACHEA
LUNGS (Excitor)
DIAPHRAGM

when you are in unfamiliar surroundings or meeting a new situation and are not sure of yourself, you close yourself up instead of opening out to others. Shy or insecure people tend to go to two extremes: either they close up and mumble or whisper, or to cover their feelings, they speak loudly, brashly and quickly, lacking the confidence which one needs to be still and listen.

Bodies reflect our mental condition. Sometimes, therefore, you can reverse the situation and try working the muscles first, and the mind will eventually accept the message. For example, the person who continually *says* he doesn't feel well, *won't* feel well. Conversely, if you speak happily, you will gradually feel happier. Try some experiments with your own voice.

4 Try saying 'Isn't it fabulous?' with your mouth turned down, your voice tuneless and your eyes staring blankly into space. It's ludicrous, isn't it? Now say: 'I've never been so happy in my life' with the same facial droop and your muscles will tone up into laughter at the incongruity.

Have you got the point?

You, and only you, can change your voice and with it your facial expression.

5 *Let's get the muscles right:*

a) First, it is a good idea to 'stand tall'. Your are worth looking at. Don't tip your head up or jut your chin. Keep your shoulders down, but not bent forward.

b) If you want to be listened to and enjoyed as a speaker you must believe in what you are saying and you must want your message to be received.

Relax the jaw; keep the cavity of the mouth, the principal resonator, as rounded and open as you can. Lips, tongue and teeth will change the shape of the resonator to produce the different vowel sounds. Pressure of lips, teeth and tongue will determine the consonants. Make a habit of opening your mouth for your voice to travel and be received.

c) Let the muscles of your lips be free and mobile. Don't cultivate the 'Englishman's stiff upper lip'. Avoid pulling the lips horizontally into a letter box slit or 'sealing' them through tension.

STAGE 2   From print to voice

Changing the meaning by varying the stress and intonation

Divide into groups of five. Each one of the group says the *same sentence* but gives it an entirely different meaning by changing the stressed word. As the stressed word changes so the 'tune' of the whole sentence changes. Notice that the stress is not made by force but by using three or four notes on one word. If you have a good ear you could try drawing a line pattern to show the compound notation (often on one word) and the subsequent notation. The descriptive phrases (a, b, c, d, e) are *not* read; they simply show you how you will interpret the sentence. (If your group consists of only three or four people use the first phrases and all have a go at the last ones.)

GROUP 1: *'I can't play in the soccer match on Friday'*

a) but my brother can.
b) however much you try to persuade me.
c) I could watch.
d) but I might play rugger.
e) but I could play on Saturday.

GROUP 2: *'Who repaired the car at Mellors' Garage?'*

a) which man was it?
b) it was a different man from the one who sold it.
c) not the bicycle.
d) when it was done elsewhere.
e) when they came home to do it.

GROUP 3: *'David won the senior swimming trophy'*

a) not Gerald.
b) he didn't just take part.
c) not the Junior.
d) not the athletics.
e) not just a certificate.

GROUP 4: *'I know John said the party was on Saturday'*

a) whatever you say.
b) I'm certain.
c) not Jane.
d) not the school play.
e) not Wednesday.

GROUP 5: *'Helen lost my library book'*

a) not Jane.
b) not just borrowed.
c) not yours.
d) not my text book.
e) not her ticket.

GROUP 6: *'Do you want to work in the holidays?'*

a) make up your mind!
b) Tim is going to.
c) are you keen to do it?
d) or play?
e) or just during the term?

Breathing

If you are healthy and breathe deeply, you will fill the *base* of your lungs and then relax the muscles so that breathing *out* is deep and thorough. If you concentrate on breathing *out* completely, nature will see that you breathe in to stay alive! If your breathing is deep and rhythmic, your voice will sound richer and you will then feel more confident. It is quite the best way of killing 'butterflies in the stomach'. We are all nervous at times.

Try to think of the voice filling the cavities of your head, face and chest, rather than throat. Any concentration on the throat will make the muscles tighter and the tone will be metallic and hard.

Volume and power

Just as your television set has a volume control so every speaker, actor, singer or reader must also control volume in relation to the listeners and the size of the room. Tune the volume and 'brilliance' of your voice so that you get a perfect relationship with your listeners. Let us begin with some sound from the whole class. See how much *power* you can get into your voice for these lines. Avoid strain or stridency.

STAGE 3   Voices for verse

You will remember the striking story in the Bible where the united shouts of the people 'brought down the walls of Jericho'. We talk of applause 'bringing the house down'. The destruction of the walls of Jericho could be a scientific fact and from what you have learned about the power of vibration in physics you will know of the powerful effect noise can have on even the most solid of objects.

(*Solo voice*) JOSHUA   Shout!
                        For the Lord has given you the city
              CROWD   So when the priests blew on their trumpets
                        The people SHOUTED.
                        When the people heard the sound of the trumpets
                        They SHOUTED with a great SHOUT
                        And / the / wall / fell / down / flat / .
                        The people went up to the city
                        Every man straight before him
                        And they took the city
                        And burned it with fire
                        And / all that was / there-in / .

In saying these words, don't just use noises, but use real power. Let every consonant hit the stones of the wall. Do you notice how many *T* sounds there are which have this **target** quality? Aim forward. Aim high. Unite your voices. Raise the eye focus. Very gradually reduce the volume and let the final line have quieter concentrated strength with slow deliberation and pauses. But keep the power and grandeur.

Now try in group speaking a modern poem on the same theme: 'The Battle of Jericho' by Valerie Lishman.

Here is a suggestion of how you could divide the poem but you may have alternative ideas. You might perhaps want to show the two alienated groups: the Israelites and the people of Jericho. On the other hand, you might want the power of all the voices for the final sounds which bring down the walls of Jericho.

(**Warning:** You had better not try 'bringing the walls down' in a room next to a class working quietly. Practise it in a hall or gym if possible.)

The Battle of Jericho

Jericho stood in the middle of the plain,	Solo 1
Stone walls glowering, high gates shut. And Joshua called on the Lord of Israel:	} All
– Help us Lord, to take this city! show us Lord, what we must do!	} Solo 2
And the Lord told Joshua how to take the city, The Lord told Joshua what to do.	} All
Seven tall priests with seven long trumpets Marched round the city with the Ark of the Covenant;	} 7 Priests
The people of Jericho climbed on the battlements, And laughed at the children of Israel.	} Group 1
The first priest puffed out his cheeks and blew	1st Priest
– Hoom boom hoom boom hoom boom hoom!	All
The second priest blew with a mighty roar	2nd Priest
– Woo wah woo wah woo wah woo!	All
The third priest gently played his part	3rd Priest
– zum zum zum zum zum zum zum!	All
The fourth priest loudly blew his horn	4th Priest
– Ra ra ra ra ra ra ra!	All
The fifth priest sounded an alarm	5th Priest
– Tan tara tan tara tan tan tara!	All
The sixth priest made a peculiar noise	6th Priest
– Kee kee kee kee kee kee kee!	All
And the seventh priest added another note	7th Priest
Ah ro ah ro ah ro ro!	All

They marched round the city with the Ark of the Covenant, And sounded the trumpets loud and clear.	} All
The people of Jericho stood on the battlements And laughed and laughed until they cried:	} Group 1
– Ho! ho! ho! ho! Ha! ha! ha! ha!	
– What a funny orchestra! Ha! ho! hee!	Solo 3
– Shall we throw some money down?	Solo 4 } from
– What d'you think they're playing at?	Solo 5 } Group 1
– Perhaps they'll blow themselves away!	Solo 6
– Ha! ho! hee!	Group 1

The seventh day came.
The children of Israel
Gathered round the city in the middle of the plain.

} Group 2

The priests took the trumpets
And prayed for victory
The Ark of the Covenant was going out to war!

} Priests

They marched round the city
And they all played together now
– Hoom boom! Woo wah! A ro! Tan tara!
  Zum zum! Kee kee! Ra ra ra!
  Ah ro! Kee kee! Zum zum! Ra ra!
  Woo wah! Hoom boom! Tan tan tara!
The children of Israel
Shouted "JEHOVAH!"
And just as the Lord said

} All

THE WALLS FELL DOWN!

Valerie Lishman

(Perhaps in the last ten lines you may want to vary the pitch and the strength through contrasted voices. You might wish, too, to use sound effects to build up the crescendo and the climax.)

Pauses creating atmosphere

Now, as a complete contrast turn the volume knob down and quietly concentrate on this incident from the book *Tarka the Otter* by Henry Williamson. At the moment of this extract of the story the hound Deadlock is drowning and people are watching the hound's body being retrieved.

Group yourselves in a fairly close huddle and decide on a focal point where the hound is drowning. Vary your levels: some kneeling, some standing, some bending down, but all looking down on the one point. Power is now in the pianissimos and the pauses – the concentrated *quietness* of your voices. In the book this passage is written in the normal prose style, but in order to show the places where pauses occur or words are sustained at the ends of lines, it is set out here like poetry.

Try it as a group reading with concentrated watching pauses, changing eye focus as the action changes.

And the tide slowed still /
and began to move back /
and they waited / and watched /
until the body of the Deadlock arose
drowned / and heavy /
and floated away
amidst the froth on the waters /

} Watch the body drown and float away

They pulled the body out of the river /
and carried it to the bank /
laying it on the grass /
and looking down at the dead hound /
in sad wonder . . . //

} *Watch the body being retrieved and hauled on to the bank*

And while they stood there silently /
a great bubble rose out of the depths /
and broke . . . //
And as they watched . . . //
another bubble shook the surface /
and broke . . . //
and there was a third bubble
in the sea-going waters . . . //
and nothing more . . . //

} *Change the eye focus back to the water and notice that although Deadlock's body is not there the water moves as if it is*

Imaginative extension of the voice by group speaking

'Behaviour of money' by Bernard Spencer is an unusual poem which lends itself to solo and group interpretation. The theme of the poem reminds us that the proverb is not: 'Money is the root of all evil' but rather 'The *love* of money is the root of all evil'. Bernard Spencer speculates on how we would behave if money died. Would we be released? or bewildered?

Behaviour of Money

All {
Money was once well known, like a townhall or the sky
or a river East and West, and you lived one side or the other;
Love and Death dealt shocks,
but for all the money passed, the wise man knew his brother.

Solo 1   But money changed. | Money came jerking roughly alive;   } *Solo 2*
went battering round the town with a boozy, zigzag tread.
Solo 3   A clear case for arrest;
All   and the crowds milled and killed for the pound notes that he shed.

Solo 4   And the town changed, | and the moan and the little lovers of gain   *Group A (light voices)*
inflated like a dropsy, | and gone were the courtesies   *Group B (dark voices)*
that eased the market day;
Group C   saying, 'buyer' and 'seller' was saying, 'enemies'.

Group A   The poor were shunted nearer to beasts. | The cops recruited.   Group B
The rich became a foreign community. | Up there leaped   } All
quiet folk gone nasty,
quite strangely disorted, like a photograph that has slipped.

All
Group A   Hearing the drunken roars of Money from down the street,
Group B {   'What's to become of us?' the people in bed would cry:
'And oh, the thought strikes chill;
what's to become of the world if Money should suddenly die?

All   Should suddenly take a toss and go down crack on his head?
Solo 5   If the dances suddenly finished, | if they stopped the runaway bus,   } Solo 6
if the trees stopped racing away?
If our hopes came true and he dies, what's to become of us?

All {   Shall we recognise each other, crowding around the body?
And as we go stealing off in search of the town we have known
– what a job for the Sanitary Officials;
the sprawled body of Money, dead, stinking, alone!'

Group A   Will X contrive to lose the weasel look in his eyes?
Group B   Will the metal go out of the voice of Y? | Shall we all turn back   Group C
to men, like Circe's beasts? |
All   Or die? Or dance in the streets the day that the world goes crack?

Bernard Spencer

Facing a Volcano

All {   Like an angry lion of the tropical jungle
The lava shoots up.
A red arrow piercing a canopy of clouds,
It threatens the endless stretch of sky.
A circling garb of hot air,
And a circling garb of humans.

Solo 1   A red cross on a green jeep,
Solo 2   A red cross on a wood shack,
Solo 3   A red cross on a white breast.
3 together {   They stand by, grim, unshaken,
To guard this circling garb of humans.

All {   They are all here.
Men, women; young and old,
Group A (light voices)   Mystified, | terrified.   Group B (dark voices)
Group A   They gape it in, | their cameras click;   Group B
All {   Later removed in space and time,
They will vent an endless chime:
'Is it not wonderful?'
Solo 4 + 5   A boy and a girl, but a few hours met,

Solos 4 + 5
Their backs to the volcano, they face the camera;
He wants a souvenir. *Solo 4*
'Is it not wonderful?' *Solo 5*
A beautiful girl, | and behind – a beautiful monster. *Group B*
Group A

Group B
A big truck unloads its cargo.
Majestic, springy, the cargo swells the circling garb of humans.
These are guards, of men against other men.
The army, of course! They too missed the red lion.

Group A No, no, this is not enemy; just a 'glorious sight'.
All And the red tongue lashes out.
Group A But it won't lick the sky;
Group B It won't lick these men – there are other tongues!

Group A What thoughts do they all have? | What feelings   *Group B*
As the eruption's bowel of lost time hurls
All The granitic deluge of suppressed earth which
Apace invades forlorn man and crop, and
Imposes a reign of barrenness;
What thoughts do they all have? What stirs them?
Group B Fear, | awe,   *Group A*
Group B Man helpless in contest with nature.
Group A He cannot harness this; | he cannot explore it.   *Group B*

All What a fire! It surpasses hell.
Solo 6 But the clergyman is not here;
Group A He has known a hell fire; | he doesn't have to see it. *Group B*
Solo 6 It is better imagined in the cloister, in the pulpit
Better described.
All Nothing real, this heat, and dust, and fire.
It makes no souls repent.

Group A They work at calculations,
Group B Scientists and seismographs.
All It defies them all, this tongue of fire, this fierce fiasco of rock and dust;
It defies time, this fiery testimony of nature.
Ruthless, devastating, defiant,
An angry arrow of fire.

Ben Mkapa

Verbal dynamism

Notice in this poem the power of the *verbs*. The verbal dynamism which creates the force of the volcano:

> shoots; piercing; threatens; lashes; lick; hurl; invades; imposes; defies.

When you are writing your own poems, strip all words away which are not 'earning their keep'. Be sparing with adjectives; and aim at imagery which makes the reader and listener have a new experience, as indeed we have in Ben Mkapa's 'Facing a volcano':

> 'a circling garb of hot air'
> 'a circling garb of humans'
> 'this fierce fiasco'
> 'angry arrow of fire'

When you are speaking the poet's words try to use your imagination as he used his, then wing the thoughts to your listeners.

The Last Flower

All	World War III, as everybody knows, Brought about the collapse of civilisation.
4 voices	Towns, cities and villages disappeared from the earth.
3 voices	All the groves and forests were destroyed
2 voices	And all the gardens
1 voice	And all the works of art.
Group B (dark voices)	Men women and children became lower than the lower animals Discouraged and disillusioned, dogs deserted their fallen masters.
Group A (light voices)	Emboldened by the pitiful condition of the former lords of the earth, Rabbits descended upon them.
All	Books, paintings and music disappeared from the earth, and human beings just sat around doing nothing.
Group A	Years and years went by
Group B	Even the few generals who were left forgot what the last war had decided.
All	Boys and girls grew up to stare at each other blankly, for love had passed from the earth.
Light solo	One day a young girl who had never seen a flower chanced to come upon the last one in the world She told the other human beings that the last flower was dying
Dark solo	The only one who paid any attention was a young man she found wandering about

Both { Together the young man and the girl nurtured the flower and it
began to live again.

Solo 3 One day a bee visited the flower, | and a humming bird.

Both { Before long there were two flowers, | and then four, and then
a great many

Solo 4
4 voices, then all

All Groves and forests flourished again

Light solo The young girl began to take an interest in how she looked

Dark solo The young man discovered that touching the girl was pleasurable

Group A Love was reborn in the world,

Group B Their children grew up strong and healthy and learned to run and laugh

Dark solo Dogs came out of their exile.

All { The young man discovered, by putting one stone upon another
how to build a shelter.

Pairs of voices for each line {
Pretty soon everybody was building shelters.
Towns, cities and villages sprang up
Song came back into the world.
And troubadours and jugglers
and tailors and cobblers
and painters and poets
and sculptors and wheelwrights
And soldiers,
And lieutenants and captains
And generals and major-generals

All And liberators

Group A Some people went one place to live, | and some another   **Group B**

Group A { Before long, those who went to live in the valleys wished they had
gone to live in the hills

Group B { And those who had gone to live in the hills wished they had gone to
live in the valleys

All {
And liberators (under the guidance of God) set fire to the discontent
So presently the world was at war again
This time the destruction was so complete . . .
That nothing at all was left in the world

Dark solo Except one man

Light solo And one woman

Both And one flower.

James Thurber

Inexpensive Progress

Group A   Encase your legs in nylons,   (Group A - light voices)
Group B   Bestride your hills with pylons   (Group B - dark voices)
All {   O age without a soul;
          Away with gentle willows
          And all the elmy billows
          That through your valleys roll.

Group A   Let's say good-bye to hedges
Group B   And roads with grassy edges
Group A   And winding country lanes;
All {   Let all things travel faster
          Where motor-car is master
          Till only Speed remains

Group A   Destroy the ancient inn-signs
Group B   But strew the roads with tin signs
3 solos   'Keep Left', | 'M4', | 'Keep Out!'
All {   Command, instruction, warning,
          Repetitive adorning
          The rockeried roundabout;

Group B { For every raw obscenity
          Must have its small 'amenity',
Group A   Its patch of shaven green,
All {   And hoardings look a wonder
          In banks of floribunda
          With floodlights in between.

Group B { Leave no old village standing
          Which could provide a landing
          For aeroplanes to roar
Group A { But spare such cheap defacements
          As huts with shattered casements
          Unlived-in since the war.

Group B { Let no provincial High Street
          Which might be your or my street
          Look as it used to do
All {   But let the chain stores place here
          Their miles of black glass facia
          And traffic thunder through.

All {   And if there is some scenery,
          Some unpretentious greenery,
          Surviving anywhere,
          It does not need protecting
          For soon we'll be erecting
          A Power Station there.

$\text{All} \left\{ \begin{array}{l} \text{When all our roads are lighted} \\ \text{By concrete monsters sited} \\ \quad \text{Like gallows overhead,} \\ \text{Bathed in the yellow vomit} \\ \text{Each monster belches from it,} \\ \quad \text{We'll know that we are dead.} \end{array} \right.$

John Betjeman

These are just suggestions for ways the poems may be divided for various voices. You may have other ideas depending on your group.

'The tower-block' by Michael Rosen is an imaginative poem for group speaking and indeed a good centrepiece for a composite documentary scene on modern inner-city building and living.

You could collect material from newspapers, reports, journals, poems and novels to make a unified miscellany and commentary on inner-city problems.

'The tower-block' shows what is lost in vertical building as compared with the old 'horizontal' neighbourly street. There are names of the street games which used to unite the street gangs. Some, you may still know, others may be known by your parents, or better still by great-grand, or grandparents, or the 'oldest inhabitants'. If you want to find out more about the games consult *Children's Games in Street and Playground* by Iona and Peter Opie (OUP, 1969).

One production of a scene based on 'The tower-block' included Patric Dickinson's poem: 'A new block'; Spike Milligan's 'Plastic woman' and Michael Rosen's 'Roads'.

The simple symbolic set was created with four grey plastic poles (drain pipes borrowed from a builder) held at the corners of the speaking group. There were a desk and chairs for the doctor and his patient for 'Roads'.

The centre front of the stage was left clear for the brief movement and 'freeze stills' of the street games. Percussion sounds were used at various points in the scene to heighten the effect and to link the items.

The scene finished with a return of the Housing Officer with the announcement and the reaction of the people.

The Tower-Block

All
> Think of this tower-block
> as if it was a street standing up
> and instead of toing and froing
> in buses and cars
> you go up and down it
> in a high speed lift.

Solo 1
> There will be no pavement artists of course
> because there aren't any pavements.

Solo 2
> There isn't room for a market
> but then there isn't room for cars.

Solo 3   No cars: | no accidents   *Solo 4*

Solo 5
> but don't lean
> out of the windows

Solo 6
> don't play in the lifts
> or they won't work

All
> They don't work
> and they won't work
> if you play | Split Kipper,   *Solo 7*

Solo 8   Fox and Chickens,
Solo 9   Dittyback,
Solo 10   Keek-bogle, | Jackerback,   *Solo 11*
Solo 12   Huckey-buck, | Hotchie-pig,   *Solo 13*
Solo 14   Foggy-plonks, | Ching Chang Cholly   *Solo 15*
Solo 16   or Bunky-Bean Bam-Bye.

All   Go down | The stairs are outside –   *Group A (light voices)*
> you can't miss them | – try not to miss them, please. } *Solo 1*
> No pets.

All
> Think how unhappy they'd be
> locked in a tower-block.

Solo 2
> There will be
> no buskers, | no hawkers   *Solo 3*

Solo 4   no flowers, | no chinwaggers,   *Solos 5 + 6*
Solos 6 + 7   no sandwich boards,
All   no passers-by
Group B   except for
(dark voices)   low-flying aircraft
Group A   or high-flying sparrows.

Solo 1
> Here is a note from Head Office:
> you will love your neighbour
> left right above below

Housing Officer
> so no music, creaky boots,
> caterwauling somersaulting –

Group B   never never never jump up or down

Group A
> or you may
> never never never get down or up again

All   No questions.

All { It's best to tip-toe,
creep, crawl, and whisper.

Housing Officer { If there are any
problems phone me
and I'll be out.
Good day.

Michael Rosen

Roads

Patient { I went to the doctor, yes,
I went to him
and I said – 'Doctor, Doctor,
it's Roads,' I said. | 'Roads?' he says.

Patient 'Roads,' I said.

Doctor 'No such thing,' he says.

Patient {
'I've got Roads, Doctor,
very bad Roads.
I've got long distance lorryworry
one way only lorry worry
They say
No U-turns Ahead.
I know I turned my head
but I saw a zebra crossing
and a bus eating a traffic jam
I can hear
unhappy new gears.
When traffic's light
at traffic lights
I see red
amber
red and amber
red already.

I wish I was a windscreen wiper
Once I washed windscreens
now I watch wipers
What shall I do?
'I've got Roads
very bad Roads, Doctor,
What shall I do?'

So he looked at me and said

Doctor { 'I don't know what I know
but I've got just the stink for you'

Patient { and he squeezed me on the Underground
And handed me the tube.

Michael Rosen

If 'The tower-block' poem is being done on its own this epilogue could follow immediately after. If a scene has been created this announcement could come at the end.

HOUSING OFFICER: Here is a note from Head Office: this building
    erected in 1970 is to be demolished because of . . .
        VOICE 1: Cracked ceiling
           2: Dry rot
           3: Rising damp
           4: Graffiti on the stairs
           5: Blocked drains
           6: Shifting steel girders
           7: Broken windows
           8: Locked lifts
           9: Unlocked doors
         10: Peeling paint
         11: Dangerous electric wiring
         12: Flats too hot in summer
         13: Flats too cold in winter
      UNISON: And no one able to love thy neighbour

        (supporting poles crash to the ground)

      UNISON: So where do we all live now?
HOUSING OFFICER: Put your name down on the waiting list and WAIT.

        (Group wander aimlessly off stage in twos and threes
        to notes of the Dead March or a minor-key pop tune)

5 You as an interviewer or an interviewee

Most schools and colleges are concerned with the local conditions of industry, the services or recreation, and the quality of, or deficiencies in, the local environment. To get to know more about the amenities and possible employment you should invite people in various positions of authority either to come and speak to you in your school or college, or try to arrange visits to the places where they operate.

Any such visit must be preceded by a courteous explanatory letter – not a telephone call. Find out the correct name and form of address of the person to whom you are writing. It is courteous to ask a busy person to come for a short session *to answer questions*; this relieves him or her of preparing a special address and has the added advantage of giving you experience in interviewing.

Planning the interview

Divide into your groups to decide whom you want to invite. Collate your suggestions and keep for future reference, but decide on one to whom you are sending a letter. (If there are five groups each making one suggestion, consult the leaders of the other groups to avoid duplication. You will thus have five speakers for the term – say, every other week.)

The letter

In your groups compose the letter and choose one representative of your group to write and sign the letter. Each letter will vary according to the particular person chosen and the 'briefing' suggested in your social studies or English course.

Here is a specimen setting out the form it might take:

Northwood County School
Southdown Road
Eastham
Date

Edward Hammond Esq
Managing Director
Isis Chemical Company
EASTHAM

Dear Mr Hammond

Members of the fifth form of our school are doing a local study of the environment which includes its industries.

As your firm is central to the economic prosperity, not only of our area but of the country, we should be so grateful if you, or a member of your staff, could visit our school to answer questions which we are composing under the following headings:

1)   Processes and production

2)   Administration and job distribution

3)   Problems affecting the environment; pollution; waste disposal; etc.

We know that you are a very busy firm and whoever comes to be interviewed by us will have little time to spare. We should, therefore, be prepared to fit in with any times you suggest either during or after school. If, however, you could choose a Friday afternoon from 3 o'clock to 4 o'clock during the next month this would fit in with our school curriculum.

We would very much appreciate your help and co-operation.

Yours sincerely

Martin Hulbert

(Written on behalf of the fifth form of Northwood County School)

This is merely an *example* of a letter and is in no sense a model to follow since every circumstance will be different.

Remember that commercial and industrial firms have little interest in creative writing or erratic and permissive spelling. They tend to judge the young, rightly or wrongly, by their basic skills. They are used to 'precision' jobs in their offices and workshops and make their judgements on these lines.

So use: correct grammar,
    correct spelling,
    courteous requests.

STAGE 2   You as the question-master

If you intend to tape-record the interview it is a courtesy to ask permission. One says things privately to a person which, when taken into another context, could be misinterpreted or misunderstood.

Appoint one of your class to be the chairman and question-master who introduces the speaker (unless your teacher wishes to do this) and calls on the members of the class, in turn and by name, to stand up and present his/her question. The questioner must speak slowly and clearly so that the question is received and remembered by the question-master and the speaker. Try to frame your questions in such a way that you give the speaker a chance to explain rather than give monosyllabic answers (*not*: 'Yes'; 'No'; a name; a date.)

a) Would you please explain how .... ?
b) Do you think that .... ?
c) How much are computers used in .... ?
d) What advice would you give .... ?

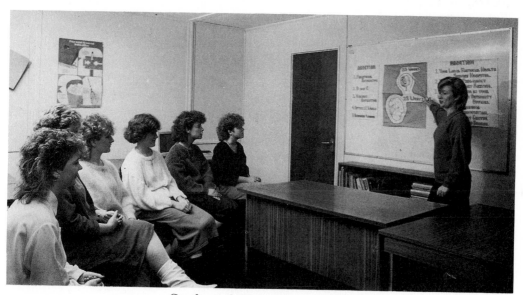

Student giving talk on abortion

e) Could you tell us what opportunities there are for young people in (bank, factory, shop, police force, council, local government, hospital, hotel, church) .... ?
f) What qualifications are required before and after having trained for .... ?

Write your questions down and make brief notes, but *say* the question looking at your visitor. Remember, though, that genuine listening will produce questions not necessarily on your list and possibly in a different order. Be flexible. React according to what you have *received*.

Your manner should be positive but not demanding or arrogant. Ask from genuine enquiry following the 'cues'.

Find out the person's name and use it in a direct, friendly way.

As you speak or listen, do make eye contact which reveals genuine warmth and interest. Much is communicated non-verbally.

Let the warmth and appreciation show in the *tone* of your voice. This will establish the 'rapport' on which all good interviewing depends.

Three or four minutes before the session is due to finish, the question-master should, after expressing his own thanks, call on a member of the listening group to give a vote of thanks on behalf of all those present.

Write a letter of thanks in which you express the benefit you have gained from the speaker's visit.

The following local organisations would be helpful in suggesting representatives of various industries and organisations:

The Rotary Club, Round Table, Business and Professional Women's Clubs, Soroptomists.

These clubs cover a wide range of male and female jobs, though few manual workers would be members. To find articulate craftsmen and 'blue-collar' workers you should keep your eyes and ears open in your own neighbourhood.

CHURCHES: You will be surprised, when you make your list, how many denominations there are. In this case you might get a panel of speakers one from each denomination and representatives of the Moslem, Buddhist, etc., fraternity in your area and through your questions find out about other people's beliefs.

POLICE: The chief constable of any town is a busy man and may not be available, but nowadays many police are trained to be able to talk about their jobs and their relationship with the community.

HEALTH SERVICE: This covers a wide range of personnel, but you could get a speaker on public health, mid-wifery, health visiting, caring for the aged, infant clinics, etc.

HOTEL AND CATERING, AND TOURIST INDUSTRY: These are 'growth' industries which offer a very wide range of jobs and careers. Sound out possible speakers through direct enquiry or the Citizens' Advice Bureau.

STORES: If your town is large enough to have a Marks and Spencer, Sainsburys or Boots (or any other multiple national store) you could sound out if they have a representative willing to come to be interviewed, alternatively you could choose a reputable local firm to speak.

BANKS: The major banks are very keen to get young people on their books. You should have no difficulty in getting a speaker after 3.30 p.m. (and possibly before) to answer your questions on all aspects of handling money.

N.B. Before you invite a speaker, get to know a definite name to whom you can address the letter personally – 'Dear Sir or Madam' letters can get short shrift in a busy office.

Introducing a speaker

Find out the following information carefully beforehand:

a) the speaker's correct name;
b) his or her past experience;
c) his or her present position and contribution to the community, industry or commerce;

When you introduce the speaker, ensure by the tone of your voice and choice of words, that your listeners feel that this is an important but *happy* occasion and that it is a unique opportunity. Give your speaker a genuine welcome and build-up.

The Chairman, having introduced the speaker, can then call the questioners. You may find after the opening questions that the questions and answers come freely and the speaker and the group can take over. Keep your eyes alert to note if anyone is being overlooked and then draw him or her in.

Vote of thanks

This cannot be prepared beforehand except in a general way. Your job is to listen to all that has been said and cite actual points you have heard that day. Remember that you are speaking on behalf of your audience, so do not introduce any controversial or contradictory remarks. Connect the audience and the speaker in your vision, but direct most of what you say to the speaker's eye and make it a short but convincing 'Thank you'.

Letter of thanks

Again (at the risk of repetition), don't forget the follow-up letter of thanks. It is doubly valuable to an adult working in your community if it comes from young people themselves and not staff.

One person can write the letter that all of the group can sign. This makes it into a letter that the recipient will appreciate. He or she will then be willing to help other groups and they will, in turn, benefit.

STAGE 3   Practice in interviewing

The aim of this role playing is to see how you can draw out the information you require and to see if you can discern the right qualities for the particular job.

Divide into groups. Your team (society, club) is advertising for a coach: a skilled adult – possibly retired – who will undertake voluntary work. Work out the plan of your interview:

Group 1: a tennis coach
Group 2: a drama coach or producer
Group 3: a philatelist for the stamp club
Group 4: a good chess player
Group 5: a video film operator

In the advertisement, which you are putting in the local press and on local radio, you should incorporate the hours, possibly days, the venue and the particular skilled help you require.

In your groups, work out the wording of the advertisement which will be read out when the class unites.

Now back in your groups compose the questions you will ask your volunteer. Exchange a person from another group with one of your team to act as an interviewee.

The interviewees will not have heard the questions.

After ten minutes the interviewees return and report to the class the arrangements which will have been made and the points which he/she will hope to work on.

Here is a checklist with the qualities you may be hoping to find in the volunteer helper. This is for your own interest and guidance. Remember you will be very lucky if you get *one* offer!

Checklist of words to help you to appreciate qualities in a good instructor.

cheerful	reliable	encouraging
optimistic	fearless	a good disciplinarian
alert	demanding	patient
challenging	fair	knowledgeable
skilful	tactful	confident
likeable	buoyant	firm

STAGE 4   You the interviewee

Presenting yourself

Your written application will give your school report with details of special courses, skills and examinations. The point of the personal interview is to find out the following:

a) your attitude to people and work
b) your practical common sense
c) your manner and ability to work with and for a team
d) your enthusiasm
e) your sincerity
f) your energy
g) your voice and speech (not *accent* but clarity and vitality)
h) your reliability
i) your adaptability
j) your conscientiousness
k) your willingness to learn.

Arrive punctually. Give yourself a few minutes in which to relax and take in your new surroundings. If you feel nervous, sit back in your chair, breathe deeply and interest yourself in people and things around you. You can learn much by your observation.

Wear clothes in which you feel comfortable but not sloppy. If they are outlandish or too new you will be consciously thinking of your 'effect' instead of listening and responding.

Creating the right atmosphere

Employers or heads of training departments are usually busy people and have only a short time in which to get to know you, so give full answers when you are spoken to. They will want to know *why* you are interested in this particular job or training. They would also like some assurance that if you are taken on that you will stay for a reasonable time.

Don't rush your answers. You will be more convincing if you *think* first and are not merely *glib*.

Don't be afraid to show that you would like to progress to a job of responsibility and that you are prepared to go through the grinding and learning processes first.

Indicate clearly if you wish to extend your knowledge or skills in further or higher education. Provision may be made for day-release or sandwich courses. It will be appreciated if you are keen enough to attend evening classes.

You will be respected if you have the right kind of ambition but not if it is merely to get the maximum money for the minimum effort. Show that you are prepared to give as well as take.

Obviously most of the questioning will be done by your prospective employer, careers officer, selection panel or personnel manager, but remember that you can ask questions too. The formalities of wages, insurance, welfare services, hours, holidays, unions, etc., should already have been explained to you, but if you want more specific details – e.g. the nature of the job, the training, or the person to whom you are responsible – then *ask*.

The interviewer will make it apparent when the interview is over and should clinch the matter by making it clear whether you will be advised of a place or whether *you* are to make up your mind and let them know. If so, fix a *time* within which you will come to a decision.

If a decision is reached at the time, make sure you are clear about the date of starting work or training and that this fits in with school and home arrangements.

Self-assessment

Most schools have elaborate marking and grading systems to assess students, but because all these letters and numbers are produced by teachers and usually record academic achievements only, you may often have had little practice in assessing yourself.

Even where you are asked to do this, as a small part of your end-of-term report or as an exercise in a non-academic lesson, you may feel that your ability begins and ends in passing exams. As earlier chapters tried to show, there are many skills and talents that schools may not value or even discover. Many can't be examined or measured – e.g. consideration for other people, enthusiasm, decisiveness, 'stickability' – but they'll all be vital for life outside school and for successful careers.

List five qualities that you see in yourself as positive and two or three that you see as weaknesses. Say where the positive qualities show up best (e.g. in a lesson, in your relationship with your friends, in your home) and how you've achieved them. Say where your weaknesses are most irritating – to you and to other people. What can you do about them? Are they all your own fault?

If you know the group you're working with well, and trust them, you could then discuss these qualities and comment on what they've said. For instance, somebody you regard as very outgoing and constructive, may describe himself as shy and nervous. The fact that you can show another side could greatly increase confidence.

Before you go to an interview, pick out from this list of words the impression that you would like to make. See how far the list tallies with your self-assessment above – if there's a lot of overlap, you should feel that you can make a good and genuine impression. If the qualities you'd like to show are quite different from your character, as you see it, be aware that you will be under strain – it may well be that you are the ideal person for the job, but poor at projecting yourself at interviews. Having thought about the good qualities you can bring to the job, you should be able to convince the interviewer that you have a lot to offer – and many of these qualities below will then start to come across, through conviction, not acting:

capable	punctual	orderly
good-humoured	unfussy	calm
adaptable	optimistic	tidy
reliable	friendly	loyal
responsible	conscientious	resourceful
practical	energetic	equable
efficient	hard-working	genuine

If you were interviewing someone for the job you're applying for or for another job that you have experienced as a consumer (e.g. teacher, doctor's reception-ist, cashier, milkman) which six qualities would you put first and why?

CHAPTER 6

You as a reader

Good reading makes great demands on any of us, as it includes many different skills. The newscasters on TV and radio, have, in a sense, been training themselves for their jobs all their lives; they still have to go on preparing and practising every day so that their work is efficiently done.

Reading aloud is a challenge to the intelligence, a test of background knowledge; it measures your ease with words, your enjoyment of them; your co-ordination of eye, brain and speech muscles and the capacity to sense your listeners' response. Reading aloud is an 'adult' accomplishment, quite different from the 'learning-to-read and being-heard' in your early years.

It is an effort which brings immediate rewards; the absorbed attention and delight of your listeners. They know and you know, without any 'marking', whether you have 'got across' or not and whether you have been able to communicate so that what you read is received and remembered by the audience.

All through life you will be trying, through various speech situations, to 'get across' to your listener in personal and professional relationships, in clubs, societies and unions. You may not have to read aloud very much, but this practice will help to give you the skill and confidence to communicate your own ideas and to hold the attention of the audience.

With experience of reading aloud your silent reading will be helped to become a rich, imaginative experience because you will see and hear the script transformed into sights and sounds.

But accepting a challenge means accepting its conditions too. To ensure good reading aloud:

a) Be familiar with your text.
b) *Share* the story, poem or play
c) Understand that the written text is a *blueprint*, like a musical score waiting for interpretation.
d) Realise that the finished product depends on the *interpreter*.
e) Accept that hearing the words is not enough for your listeners; the expression in your eyes will communicate meaning too.

Think of the skill you use in working from a technical drawing to a solid model in metal or wood; or the difference between the paper dress pattern and the finished model 'in the round' with its interesting cut, texture and movement.

This is how you should think of a printed story, novel, play or poem. It is not a question of making silent reading audible, but of creating a three-dimensional, hi-fi, animated 'happening' and making it happen *now*. To get this effect, you will need variety in:

rhythm, stress, volume, pace and pause.

STAGE 1   Facing your listeners

Stand tall with your weight on both feet. This gives you more power in your voice and breath support. Your listeners, too, feel that you have more confidence and authority.

Your eyes should go ahead and scan the whole phrase or sentence, find whole 'thinking chunks'. This 'thinking chunk' is what you have to get across to your listeners.

Dialogue very often precedes the 'signal' word which tells you *how* to say the words: 'shouted', 'screamed', 'yelled', 'whispered', 'commanded', etc. So your eyes must go ahead to discover the signal word before you say the dialogue. Notice the 'signal' words in the *Catch 22* extract (page 83) and in the *Golden Horseshoe* (page 91) and *Memories of Christmas* (page 88).

Your eyes should reflect the mood or thought so that your listeners are also *viewers*. You are your own best audio-visual aid.

You will need pauses for reflection and your listeners will need pauses for reception. In this way you share the message with them.

Your voice should create the different characters and atmosphere, and be projected in such a way that every single listener receives your message and *remembers* it.

The way you change *pace* from bottom gear to top gear will change the atmosphere and the scene. The story must happen *now* and it must move away from the printed page.

Try out these ideas so that everyone at some time in the term has a chance to be a 'professional' reader.

STAGE 2   Reading and listening in a small group

Work in groups of four or five. Each group selects a different episode from a book which all have read. Divide the episode between you so that each one has 90–120 seconds reading time. Read your part of the story thoroughly, getting any necessary help with the meaning of the words and their pronunciation. You will then discover changes of pace, pitch, pause and pressure. After five minutes combine and read the passage aloud in sequence, making the story as vivid as you can.

Now give as much constructive criticism as possible to one another.

a) Which passages were interesting to listen to?
b) Which ones will you *remember*?
c) Could certain phrases have been made more memorable? Which ones? If so, how?

Re-uniting groups for class comment: The individual groups now become a focal point for the rest of the class. The first reader introduces the passage putting into practice all the suggestions received earlier. The other readers follow in succession, making firm contact with the listening group. In this way larger parts of the texts will be covered and the effort will be enjoyed by readers and listeners.

Class comments and evaluation:

a) Did the readers hold our attention?
b) Was the 'atmosphere' of the text created?
c) Did the dialogue sound like real conversation?
d) Did the readers speak with their *eyes*?
e) Did they share the story?
f) What phrases were made memorable?

Subsequent teams will then read, though not necessarily in the same session.

Reading from a book the whole group have studied

Joseph Heller's *Catch 22* describes the nightmare logic of war, where pilots have to fly endless missions until they protest that it's crazy to go on flying them. This protest proves their sanity – so they are compelled to continue on the bombing missions – Catch 22. There are many vivid, violent and, at times, horrific accounts of the chaos on the ground and in the air.

In this section, Yossarian, the central character, is trying to guide his pilot, McWatt, out of the anti-aircraft barrage which has suddenly hit them. The navigator, Aarfy, should be helping, but he is just enthralled by the sight of so much anti-aircraft fire and he stands around placidly, getting in everyone's way. So the passage alternates between his crazy calm and enormous bursts of energy and danger, as Yossarian desperately tries to save himself and his plane.

'Will you get out of here?' he yelped beseechingly, and shoved Aarfy over with all his strength. 'Are you deaf or something? Get back in the plane!' And to McWatt he screamed, 'Dive! *Dive!*'.

Down they sank once more into the crunching, thudding, voluminous barrage of bursting anti-aircraft shells as Aarfy, came creeping back behind   5

Yossarian and jabbed him sharply in the ribs again. Yossarian shied upward with another whinnying gasp.

'I still couldn't hear you,' Aarfy said.

'I said get out of here!' Yossarian shouted, and broke into tears. He began punching Aarfy in the body with both hands as hard as he could. 'Get away from me! Get away!'

Punching Aarfy was like sinking his fists into a limp sack of inflated rubber. There was no resistance, no response at all from the soft, insensitive mass, and after a while Yossarian's spirit died and his arms dropped helplessly with exhaustion. He was overcome with a humiliating feeling of impotence and was ready to weep in self-pity.

'What did you say?' Aarfy asked.

'Get away from me,' Yossarian answered, pleading with him now, 'Go back in the plane.'

'I still can't hear you.'

'Never mind,' wailed Yossarian, 'never mind. Just leave me alone.'

'Never mind what?'

Yossarian began hitting himself in the forehead. He seized Aarfy by the shirt front and, struggling to his feet for traction, dragged him to the rear of the nose compartment and flung him down like a bloated and unwieldy bag in the entrance of the crawlway. A shell banged open with a stupendous clout right beside his ear as he was scrambling back toward the front, and some undestroyed recess of his intelligence wondered that it did not kill them all. They were climbing again. The engines were howling again as though in pain, and the air inside the plane was acrid with the smell of machinery and fetid with the stench of gasoline. Then next thing he knew, it was snowing!

Thousands of tiny bits of white paper were falling like snow-flakes inside the plane, milling around his head so thickly that they clung to his eyelashes when he blinked in astonishment and fluttered against his nostrils and lips each time he inhaled. When he spun round in bewilderment, Aarfy was   35
grinning proudly from ear to ear like something inhuman as he held up a shattered paper map for Yossarian to see. A large chunk of flak had ripped up from the floor through Aarfy's colossal jumble of maps and had ripped out through the ceiling inches away from their heads. Aarfy's joy was sublime.

'Will you look at this?' he murmured, waggling two of his stubby fingers   40
playfully into Yossarian's face through the hole in one of his maps. 'Will you look at this?'

Yossarian was dumbfounded by his state of rapturous contentment. Aarfy was like an eerie ogre in a dream, incapable of being bruised or evaded, and Yossarian dreaded him for a complex of reasons he was too petrified to   45
untangle. Wind whistling up through the jagged gash in the floor kept the myriad bits of paper circulating like alabaster particles in a paperweight and contributed to a sensation of lacquered, waterlogged unreality. Everything seemed strange, so tawdry and grotesque. His head was throbbing from a shrill clamor that drilled relentlessly into both ears. It was McWatt, begging   50
for directions in an incoherent frenzy. Yossarian continued staring in tormented fascination at Aarfy's spherical countenance beaming at him so serenely and vacantly through the drifting whorls of white paper bits and concluded that he was a raving lunatic just as eight bursts of flak broke open successively at eye level off to the right, then eight more, and then eight   55
more, the last group pulled over toward the left so that they were almost directly in front.

'Turn left hard!' he hollered to McWatt, as Aarfy kept grinning, and McWatt did turn left hard, but the flak turned left hard with them, catching up fast, and Yossarian hollered, 'I said hard, hard, hard, hard, you bastard,   60
hard!'

And McWatt bent the plane around even harder still, and suddenly, miraculously, they were out of range. The flak ended. The guns stopped booming at them. And they were alive.

Joseph Heller, *Catch 22*

When you are preparing a piece to read, it's worth tackling in the most microscopic detail. Mark words that need emphasis or special care; move on to larger units that must be said with a particular stress or tone; then decide where the spaces are for breath.

Vary the pace, so that the listener is never predicting your next few sentences. Vary the intensity – even in such a dramatic piece, a hammering delivery would quickly put the audience off. Finally, see if the overall shape of your reading has pace and varied interest.

The tempo of this piece depends very much on alternate explosions and exhaustions.

You will have to find what suits your style of delivery best, but here are a few suggestions:

Lines 1–3: Before you start, let your eye go ahead to the signal word: 'beseechingly' then an abrupt and loud start, but not full power, as you have to go from a line that is 'yelped' to one that is 'screamed', and the second 'Dive!', as the italics show, must be even more urgent than the first.

Lines 4–7: A lot of sound effects that need plenty of breath control and careful pacing, as they pile up – 'crunching, thudding, voluminous barrage of bursting anti-aircraft shells'. This may leave your audience breathless, but it mustn't leave you breathless, too. You can then slow for the moment for 'Aarfy came creeping back' and speed up on 'jabbed him sharply.' Try to give the full big sound effect of 'whinnying gasp'.

Lines 8–11: Change the voice and tempo to the insanely relaxed and complacent remark 'I still couldn't hear you' before switching back to the desperate and growing urgency of 'I said get *out of here*!'. Notice that '*out*' is more important than get, whereas 'get out' would usually be said in one breath with equal emphasis. Yossarian is already starting to be powerless and sob rather than shout, 'Get *away* from me! Get *away*!', because any energy his fear leaves him is going into hitting Aarfy.

Lines 12–16: Two fairly short sentences frame a long one in this paragraph. Therefore, try to 'hinge' this section round the moment in the middle where Yossarian has thrown himself with every ounce of strength at a man he can't really affect at all – e.g. fast and purposeful delivery on 'no resistance, no response at all from the soft, insensitive mass, and after a while . . .' come down from this crescendo to a slower, more resigned tone.

Lines 17–22: This repeats the maddening conversation at the start, but it mustn't seem the same. Yossarian's lines are 'pleading' so the contrast is not between complacency (Aarfy) and anger (Yossarian), but perhaps a genuine concern on Aarfy's part to hear Yossarian properly, contrasted with an appealing warmth in Yossarian's voice to get through to Aarfy.

Lines 23–31: Mark the stages in the growing danger here – first the success of finally moving Aarfy, undercut by the shock effect of a shell *banged* open with a *stupendous* clout; then the balanced sentence of 'acrid with the smell of machinery' and 'fetid with the stench of gasoline'. Still have enough in reserve to convey the amazement at the end: 'it was snowing'.

Lines 32–39: The chaos becomes like a dream. As this ends in Aarfy's joy, it can be read in a much more fairy-tale tone, as though everything is beautiful and reassuring.

Lines 40–42: Aarfy's words develop this feeling of childish delight – if you can chortle or even gurgle them and make them audible, this would convey what Yassarian feels – he is dealing with a mad ogre.

Lines 43–56: The longest paragraph in the extract, with the most danger. Up to line 49, time seems to stand still, so you can place this steadily and concentrate on the intricate detail – there are several tongue-twisters – e.g.

'alabaster particles in a paperweight'. Notice the short sentences (e.g. line 48) varying the rhythm too. The last sentence is very long and needs to be carefully marked up, so that you can sustain the momentum for eight lines, which must also be delivered to convey the universal feeling of danger and chaos.

Lines 57–62: Life-saving commands are 'hollered', so this should probably be the loudest and most distraught delivery of any dialogue building to a climax in line 59. Then the sentences, though two start with 'and', calm down, slow down and separate into simple, relieved statements, so that the final four words ought to come across as a stark and almost wondering contrast to all the catalogue of violence and confusion before them.

STAGE 3   Winning an audience

At home, or in your private study period, choose an exciting paragraph from a book you have thoroughly enjoyed. Work on it until you can transmit that enjoyment to your whole class. When it is your turn – this may not come until later in the term – introduce the book and the author clearly and give a persuasive, enthusiastic comment on your choice, before actually reading it aloud. The test of your success will be how many of the class want to borrow the book for reading.

It is an excellent way of recommending books to other people.

Choosing a passage

The first requirement is that you choose something you enjoy and that you want other people to enjoy and respond to. As long as the passage is vivid and memorable, it needn't be an official classic or be full of difficult words. Examiners who have heard many readings by many different sorts of students will all come up with different favourites – from modern popular bestsellers like *Christine* by Stephen King, to a famous piece of historical description, like Plato's account of the death of Socrates. You may get some useful ideas from hearing works well read on television and radio (*Book at Bedtime*, *The Morning Story*, *Jackanory* Schools' broadcasting – your school may have back numbers of the excellent series, *Listening and Writing* or *Books, Plays and Poems*, published by the BBC, where self-contained extracts may save you the trouble of editing a good piece out of a long chapter: you should still read the rest of the book so that you can explain the characters' backgrounds and the story so far.)

Nearly all publishers produce interesting anthologies of writing on particular themes – e.g. *The Penguin English Project* (now published by Ward Lock Educational) has a wide range of short but striking passages on a huge number of themes. Some of the best 'audition pieces' may be fairly familiar to your audience, so, although there's nothing wrong with choosing a piece from *Kes* by Barry Hines or one of Roald Dahl's books, it may be worth looking round for less well-known passages. Asking friends, teachers, parents, librarians what their favourite books are will extend your own reading, even if you don't find exactly the piece you want straight away.

Here is an incident, complete in itself, from *Memories of Christmas* by Dylan Thomas. Read it silently first and you'll soon see that it must be read *aloud*!

If you can give Mrs Prothero a gong to bang, the word 'Fire' is going to burst in your listeners' ears. You might, after solo readings, try it out as a dramatised scene with a narrator; whichever way you do it the action and excitement should arrest and amuse your listeners.

MEMORIES OF CHRISTMAS

'Fire!' cried Mrs Prothero, and she beat the dinner-gong. And we ran down the garden, with the snowballs in our arms, towards the house, and smoke, indeed, was pouring out of the dining-room, and the gong was bombilating, and Mrs Prothero was announcing ruin like a town-crier. This was better than all the cats in Wales standing on the wall in a row. We bounded into the house, laden with snowballs, and stopped at the open door of the smoke-filled room. Something was burning all right; perhaps it was Mr Prothero, who always slept there after midday dinner with a newspaper over his face; but he was standing in the middle of the room, saying 'A fine Christmas!' and smacking at the smoke with a slipper.

'Call the fire-brigade', cried Mrs Prothero as she beat the gong. There was no fire to be seen, only clouds of smoke and Mr Prothero standing in the middle of them, waving his slipper as though he were conducting.

'Do something,' he said.

And we threw all our snowballs into the smoke – I think we missed Mr Prothero – and ran out of the house to the telephone-box.

'Let's call the police as well,' Jim said.

'And the ambulance.'

'And Ernie Jenkins, he likes fires.'

But we only called the fire-brigade, and soon the fire-engine came and three tall men in helmets brought a hose into the house and Mr Prothero got out just in time before they turned it on. Nobody could have had a noisier Christmas Eve.

Dylan Thomas, *Memories of Christmas*

Your own choice of book

As this will probably be completely new to your audience, you have to give everybody more background than for the first method. A poem, by a writer like Seamus Heaney, who specialises in sharp impressions in beautifully crafted, echoing language, may be an appropriate stimulus. It is brief but dramatic, rhythmical and full of strong sounds. 'A Constable Calls' takes you straight into a childhood memory of Heaney's – the local policeman checking on his father's accounts of what grew in his fields. The poem has a more general point too; it suggests the threatening presence of an outsider, who has the power to arrest and imprison anyone ('the black hole in the barracks') – at least in the child's imagination, which turns the policeman's bicycle into a huge, menacing machine. The delicate details add up the sense of 'Arithmetic and fear' and should lead to an interesting discussion of people and things which seem frightening when you're small and over-awed by their power.

A Constable Calls

His bicycle stood at the window-sill,
The rubber cowl of a mud-splasher
Skirting the front mudguard,
Its fat black handlegrips

Heating in sunlight, the 'spud'
Of the dynamo gleaming and cocked back,
The pedal treads hanging relieved
Of the boot of the law.

His cap was upside down
On the floor, next his chair.
The line of its pressure ran like a bevel
In his slightly sweating hair.

He had unstrapped
The heavy ledger, and my father
Was making tillage returns
In acres, roods, and perches.

Arithmetic and fear.
I sat staring at the polished holster
With its buttoned flap, the braid cord
Looped into the revolver butt.

'Any other root crops?
Mangolds? Marrowstems? Anything like that?'
'No,' But was there not a line
Of turnips where the seed ran out

In the potato field? I assumed
Small guilts and sat
Imagining the black hole in the barracks.
He stood up, shifted the baton-case

Further round on his belt,
Closed the domesday book,
Fitted his cap back with two hands,
And looked at me as he said goodbye.

A shadow bobbed in the window.
He was snapping the carrier spring
Over the ledger. His boot pushed off
And the bicycle ticked, ticked, ticked.

Seamus Heaney

This is part of a longer sequence of poems called 'Singing School' in Heaney's collection, *North*. He begins this with a quotation from Wordsworth's poem 'The Prelude' including the lines 'I grew up / Fostered alike by beauty and by fear'. Where you grew up and the impressions your surroundings made on you can help you decide what sort of passage to choose. A West Country voice reading Laurie Lee's *Cider with Rosie*, or a Manchester voice reading Robert Roberts' *A Ragged Schooling*, or a Suffolk voice reading Robert Blythe's *Akenfield* (see page 44) will not only be appropriate but you will probably fall naturally into the speech patterns of the author.

STAGE 4   Professional storytelling

In your separate groups, prepare a story between you which you could read to primary-school children, a class with special needs, or those who have reading difficulties. Get help from the staff to choose an appropriate story. If it is told well you might even want to record it on tape, keeping it for future use. People with difficulty in reading could then play the soundtrack, while following the story on the printed page. Your class could produce five or six cassettes which would be invaluable to struggling readers. Remember that to be good enough for the children, you must be excellent!

A story for children

Patrick Duggan's *The Golden Horseshoe* has some classic ingredients of a good children's story; a good but unconventional group of outsiders (the tinkers,) a girl (Sharon) who is transported to a magic land where she falls into the power of a wicked enchanter (Balor). In this extract, the tinkers use the enchanter's powerful Evil Eye to break down the walls of the gaolhouse, where many of their friends have been locked up. Balor is particularly bad-tempered because he's lost his clothes and been confined to a bath for transport; Sharon now has him in her power because she has the magic whistle, which he must obey wherever he is, and whatever he's doing. Balor, Sharon and the other tinkers wait while Old Mag goes up to the gaolhouse, to see if she can get inside and warn the prisoners to get ready to escape.

Old Mag picked up a stone and banged on the door. The sound echoed eerily inside. She watched a moment then banged again. She could hear the clank of keys and heavy footsteps approaching on the other side. She held her breath as the door creaked open. It was all she could do not to turn and run at the sight of the ugly rough face of the gaoler who looked out at her. However, she managed to smile and dropped a curtsey.
'Good day to you, your honour,' she began. 'I'm just a poor tinker woman come to see me tribe who you've got locked up inside. If you'd let me in to see them may the blessing of Almighty God and his sanctified saints be on you this day . . .'
   'And the devil blast you, if you don't,' she added under her breath.
   The gaoler glared at her for a while as though he couldn't make up his mind. Then he grunted and, stepping back, held the door open and beckoned with his head for her to enter. She smiled and dropped another curtsey and went inside. The door clanked shut behind her.
   'Well so far, so good,' said Usheen, watching with the rest of them through the bushes. Suddenly Skipeen started to whimper.
   'What's the matter?' Maeve asked. 'My foot's gone to sleep,' he said, hopping about. 'Well, waken it,' said Maeve. 'He's always the same,' Balor complained.

There was silence amongst them again. 'I'm frightened,' said Sharon. Usheen put his arm around her. They all watched anxiously for Old Mag's signal.

'There it is!' Maeve broke in. Sure enough, Old Mag's piece of red cloth fluttered through the bars of the prison window.

'Quickly!' said Usheen pushing the bath out into the open from the bushes. They all followed him. 'The bath is almost slipping down the hill,' he gasped. 'Help me, Skipeen.'

The little fella grabbed hold of the bath with Usheen.

Maeve waved her sword threateningly at Balor. 'Now!' she commanded.

Balor looked down at the wall of the gaolhouse and slowly took the patch away from his Evil Eye. A beam of vivid blue light shot out from it; there was a rumbling sound as part of the gaolhouse wall crumbled away.

'We've done it!' Skipeen cheered as the tinkers poured through the gap in the wall. Up the hill they ran, Rory almost dragging Old Mag behind him.

Sharon rushed to him and threw her arms about him. He hugged her and swung her round. 'Why some of them are only children,' Neeve said surprised, as the tinkers scrambled up the hill.

There was a roar as the great iron door swung open and the gaolers ran out in pursuit. 'Action stations!' Maeve shouted with sword and shield at the ready. Usheen ran to her side.

'I can't hold this on me own,' Skipeen screamed, struggling with the bath, which was starting to slip down the hill again. 'Where's that ole faggot with the clothes?' Balor roared.

'Get back to the camp as quickly as possible,' Usheen called to the tinkers.

'Look out!' Maeve screamed at him. Looking round he saw one of the gaolers taking a leap at him. He dodged to one side and the gaoler landed . . . splash . . . in the bath on top of Balor. Skipeen reeled back in shock and lost his grip.

The extra weight caused the bath to slide downhill at great speed, with Balor and the gaoler roaring at the tops of their voices. Down, down, down it sped, careering straight towards the door of the gaol. Just as it reached the doorway a group of gaolers came running out to help recapture the tinkers. Crash . . . splash . . . ooohhh. The bath upturned in the middle of them, pitching Balor and the gaoler into the air.

Skipeen watched with delight as they all slipped and slithered on the ground. Balor was frantically trying to cover himself with suds again.

'What a mess,' the little fella commented. 'They'll all need a bath after that lot!'

Patrick Duggan, *The Golden Horseshoe*

STAGE 5   Presenting your own programme

Work out an assembly programme on a chosen *theme*, together with your classmates, using extracts of poems, stories, novels, newspaper accounts, diaries, etc. Practise reading so that your voice can be heard at the back of the school hall, and so that you are so familiar with the script that you can pause and 'share' with your eyes focussed on the listeners.

A chosen theme

One of the most famous 'readers' of all times was Charles Dickens. His popular readings from his works were electrifying and used up so much of his energy that he probably shortened his life by his hectic programme of public appearances. A collection of his 'hits' can be found in *Sykes and Nancy* edited by Phil Collins. This includes some excellent sequences from *Oliver Twist*, *Hard Times* and *Nicholas Nickleby*, among other books. You may find these selections (though far too long for normal modern readings) interesting for their choice of climaxes and gestures (Dickens left many stage directions for his own performances). Dickens lends himself to dramatisation with different actors performing his words, as the Royal Shakespeare Company's adaptation of *Nicholas Nickleby* showed. If you are interested in the massive problems that were overcome by the adaptor, David Edgar, the producer, Trevor Nunn, and the company, Leon Rubin's account is extremely interesting (*The Story of Nicholas Nickleby*). Many other dramatic adaptations have been made, from Lionel Bart's musical *Oliver* to the latest BBC serial version of *Bleak House*.

In this extract – which could easily be divided between different speakers and a narrator – Jo, the crossing-sweeper, in *Bleak House*, who has been a key witness to events which he doesn't understand, including guiding a mysterious lady to a squalid cemetery, is being looked after by the surgeon, Allan Woodcourt. Jo is very ill, and terrified of being 'moved on' yet again – the only home he has ever known is the filthy, broken-down tenement called Tom-all-Alone's. Dickens' indignation at the sufferings of poor, homeless people like Jo links with earlier criticism of the grand lords and politicians who do nothing to improve the plight of thousands of Londoners.

Jo is in a sleep or in a stupor to-day, and Allan Woodcourt, newly arrived, stands by him, looking down upon his wasted form. After a while, he softly seats himself upon the bedside with his face towards him – just as he sat in the law-writer's room – and touches his chest and heart. The cart had very nearly given up, but labours on a little more.

The trooper stands in the doorway, still and silent. Phil has stopped in a low clinking noise, with his little hammer in his hand. Mr Woodcourt looks round with that grave professional interest and attention on his face, and, glancing significantly at the trooper, signs to Phil to carry his table out. When the little hammer is next used, there will be a speck of rust upon it.

'Well, Jo! What is the matter? Don't be frightened.'

'I thought,' says Jo, who has started, and is looking round, 'I thought I was in Tom-all-Alone's agin. Ain't there nobody here but you, Mr Woodcot?'

'Nobody.'

'And I ain't took back to Tom-all-Alone's. Am I, sir?'

'No.' Jo closes his eyes, muttering, 'I'm wery thankful.'

After watching him closely a little while, Allan puts his mouth very near his ear, and says to him in a low, distinct voice:

'Jo! Did you ever know a prayer?'

'Never knowd nothink, sir.'

'Not so much as one short prayer?'

'No, sir. Nothink at all. Mr Chadbands he wos a-prayin wunst at Mr Sangsby's and I heerd him, but he sounded as if he wos a-speakin to hisself, and not to me. He prayed a lot, but *I* couldn't make out nothink on it. Different times, there wos other genlmen come down Tom-all-Alone's a-prayin, but they all mostly sed as the t'other wuns prayed wrong, and all mostly sounded to be a-talkin to theirselves, or a-passin blame on the t'others, and not a-talkin to us. *We* never knowd nothink. *I* never knowd what it wos all about.'

It takes him a long time to say this; and few but an experienced and attentive listener could hear, or, hearing, understand him. After a short relapse into sleep or stupor, he makes, of a sudden, a strong effort to get out of bed.

'Stay, Jo! What now?'

'It's time for me to go to that there berryin-ground, sir,' he returns, with a wild look.

'Lie down, and tell me. What burying-ground, Jo?'

'Where they laid him as wos very good to me, wery good to me indeed, he wos. It's time fur me to go down to that there berryin-ground, sir, and ask to be put along with him. I wants to go there and be berried. He used fur to say to me, "I am as poor as you to-day, Jo," he ses. I wants to tell him that I am as poor as him now, and have come there to be laid along with him.'

'By-and-bye, Jo. By-and-bye.'

'Ah! P'raps they wouldn't do it if I wos to go myself. But will you promise to have me took there, sir, and laid along with him?'

'I will, indeed'.

'Thank-ee, sir. Thank'ee, sir. They'll have to get the key of the gate afore they can take me in, for it's allus locked. And there's a step there, as I used fur to clean with my broom – It's turned wery dark, sir. Is there any light a-coming?'

'It is coming fast, Jo.'

Fast. The cart is shaken all to pieces, and the rugged road is very near its end.

'Jo, my poor fellow!'

'I hear you sir, in the dark, but I'm a-gropin-a-gropin- let me catch hold of your hand.'

'Jo, can you say what I say?'

'I'll say anythink as you say sir, fur I know it's good.'

'OUR FATHER.'

'Our Father! – yes, that's wery good, sir.'

'WHICH ART IN HEAVEN.'

'Art in Heaven – is the light a-comin, sir?'

'It is close at hand. HALLOWED BE THY NAME!'

'Hallowed be-thy-'

The light is come upon the dark benighted way.   Dead! Dead, your Majesty. Dead, my lords and gentlemen.   Dead, Right Reverends and Wrong Reverends of every order.   Dead, men and women, born with Heavenly compassion in your hearts. And dying thus around us every day.

Charles Dickens, *Bleak House*

This extract could be part of a 'Victorian cities' or poverty theme. For the Victorian city presentation, there are a wide range of different types of reading available – documentary accounts from Mayhew's *London Labour* and *London Poor*, street ballads, contemporary accounts of the Great Exhibition, Victorian melodramas and so on. A poverty theme means that you can extend your range of readings through a wide variety of cultures – e.g. Oscar Lewis' *Children of Sanchez*, modern treatments like Jeremy Sandford's *Cathy Come Home*, Orwell's *Down and Out in Paris and London*, poems from Blake's *London* to Adrian Mitchell's *For Beauty Douglas*, documentary evidence from Shelter and other organisations like the Child Poverty Action Group – the range is limited only by your own time for research.

STAGE 6   Reviewing and assessing your performance

When your reading has become good enough you can move from school audiences to semi-public ones. Get in touch with children needing special help with their reading, children with physical or mental handicaps. Offer your services to blind people singly or in Homes. You will easily see if you are getting across to your listeners by their attention and you will be able to face 'public speaking' with increasing confidence.

Give yourself a thorough check-up before meeting your listeners. Are you making the best of yourself? Ask yourself:

a) Do I fully understand the passage and the words?

b) Have I grouped the words into complete thoughts?

c) Have I discovered pauses, other than commas and full stops?

d) How have I *emphasised* necessary points, making the text come alive?

    1) with change of volume?

    2) with change of pace?

    3) with eye-contact?

    4) with change of tone?

    5) with change of facial expression?

e) If there are different characters in the reading, do they *sound* different?
f) Will the listeners *remember* what I have read?

For the most public form of reading, you need to have experimented with readings before a small, sympathetic audience, to see what holds people's attention and what doesn't. Any of the approaches listed above may develop into a powerful and entertaining series of readings, whether based on a theme (like war), a period (like Victorian), a genre (like autobiography) or a particular place (like Northern Ireland or the West Country or, clearly one of the richest sources of literature, The Lakes, admirably covered in Norman Nicholson's Penguin anthology of the same name). It may be that a culture and an activity that is totally unfamiliar to your listeners will be as gripping to hear described, as familiar experiences. It all depends on the quality of the writing. This final extract is beautifully written, deals with a magical world and has intricate attention to detail – so it would fit the theme of work, the world of a child's imagination, a collection of autobiographical pieces or a look at unusual places and periods that have vanished for ever.

Read it silently first and work on it till you feel that the words belong to you. Later you can read it in a small group, if necessary dividing it into paragraphs, one for each speaker, and see whether you can convey its power. Then you can judge whether it will fit a more public reading.

My Father's Skill

It occurred to me later that my father could easily have relinquished all the work of smelting gold to one or other of his assistants: they were not without experience in these matters: they had taken part hundreds of times in the same preparations and they would certainly have brought the work to a successful conclusion. But as I have told you, my father kept moving his lips! We could not hear the words, those secret words, those incantations which he addressed to powers that we should not, that we could not hear or see; this was essential. Only my father was versed in the science of conjuring the spirits of fire, air or gold, and conjuring evil spirits, and that is why he alone conducted the whole operation.

By now the gold would have cooled in the hollow of the brick, and my father would begin to hammer and stretch it. This was the moment when his work as a goldsmith really began.

The woman for whom the trinket was being made, and who would often have looked in to see how the work was getting on, would come for the final time, not wanting to miss anything of the marvellous sight as the gold wire, which my father had succeeded in spinning, was transformed into a trinket. She was here now, devouring with her eyes the fragile golden wire, following its tranquil and inevitable spirals round the little metal cone which gave the trinket its shape.

My father would be watching her out of the corner of his eye, and sometimes I would see the corners of his mouth twitch into a smile: the woman's avid attentiveness amused him.

'Are you trembling?' he would say to her.

'*Am* I trembling?' she would ask.

And we would all burst out laughing at her. For she *was* trembling, with covetousness for the spiral pyramid in which my father was inserting, among the convolutions, tiny grains of gold. When finally he terminated the work by placing at the summit the largest grain of gold, the woman would jump excitedly to her feet.

Then, while my father was slowly turning the trinket round in his fingers, smoothing it into perfect shape, no one could have displayed such utter happiness as the native woman, not even the praise-singer, whose trade it was to do so, and who, during the whole process of transformation, had kept on singing his praises, accelerating his rhythm, increasing his flatteries as the trinket took shape, and praising my father's talents to the skies.

Indeed the praise-singer participated in a curious – I was going to say direct, effective – way in the work. He, too, was intoxicated with the job of creation; he declaimed his rapture, and plucked his harp like a man inspired; he warmed to the task as if he had been the craftsman himself, as if the trinket had been made by his own hands. He was no longer a paid thurifer;* he was no longer just the man whose services each and anyone could hire: he became a man who creates his song under the influence of some very personal, interior necessity.

When my father, after having soldered the large grain of gold that crowned the summit, held out his work to be admired, the go-between would no longer be able to contain himself, and would intone the douga – the great chant which is only sung for celebrated men, and which is danced to only for them.

At the first notes of the douga my father would rise and utter a cry in which happiness and triumph were equally mingled; and brandishing in his right hand the hammer that was the symbol of his profession, and in his left a ram's horn filled with magic substances, he would dance the glorious dance.

Camara Laye, *The Dark Child*

*****thurifer:** person who carries a censer usually holding incense.

7 Preparing and presenting your personal project

STAGE 1 Individual projects

1 Your personal project

Choose a subject which is of real interest to you and one in which you have done, or intend to do, practical work or research. Live with it for some time. If you choose a personal project related to your school work for GCSE or ESB examination, select a section which is enhanced by visual and oral presentation. Do not try to cover too wide an aspect of the work but rather take one section of the subject on which you have done some personal research in depth. Remember that you are then entitled to be the person in authority.

Present your exposition in a colourful, graphic way so that it will be remembered. Give actual demonstrations where relevant.

Finally, relax and *share*. Giving a talk on something personally achieved brings your whole personality into play. It shows your enthusiasm, friendliness, curiosity, discovery, adventure, 'guts', humility, originality, good humour and wit. Notice 'humility'. Although you are in a position of authority and are being treated as such – somewhere, amongst your listeners there may be people who know more about the subject than you do. So show your sources of information and give tribute to the people who have helped or inspired you. Don't hesitate to say if you don't know the answer to a question; you might be able to suggest where your enquirer could go for more authoritative information or you might profit from your questioner's experience.

2 Presentation

Remember that if your talk is for group presentation, every listener is also a *viewer*. Enlarge your diagrams or pictures and use a bold black felt pen for the outlines. If your visual aids are well thought out and presented they can also be your note-headings, leaving you free to talk. Your eye will be free too, to make direct contact with the exhibits and the audience. If notes are used, then they should be headings for reference only, and not an essay for continuous reading or memorised repetition.

Think out ways in which your charts, pictures and equipment are to be quickly and effectively put into position. Arrange for a colleague to 'stage-manage' for you. You can then do the same in return.

3 Contact with your audience

a) Stand 'tall'; glance round so that you have caught each member of the group with your eye. Make sure that you have everyone 'with you' before you begin.

b) Leave your hands completely free and relaxed so that they are ready when you want to point to a picture or a diagram. If they are free, they will move as your thoughts change so that almost unconsciously you will be communicating with significant gesture.

c) Remember that you are a *person* and not a text book. If you have personal experience related to your subject let this come through at the beginning. If your audience feels that you have genuine enthusiasm, having discovered and tested things *yourself*, they will be much more interested than if you give a factual account as if from an encyclopaedia or text book.

d) If you have dates, figures or names to get across, say them very slowly and deliberately, repeating them if you think it necessary, or have them set out beforehand on a chart, in bold type. Remember that your listeners may be hearing these facts for the first time. Make sure they receive and remember the facts by using graphic analogy.

   For example, it is more arresting to say 'capture the power of one flash of lightning and you could light one million electric bulbs', than to give a long mathematical equation with numbers which cannot be remembered.

e) Try to include every individual member of the group in your vision at some time so that no one feels left out. You should be 'telling' not 'reciting'.

f) Project your voice so that it is easy for those on the back row, or furthest away from you to hear. The ideal arrangement is a single or double horseshoe of chairs, not desks, with the speakers and their props in the open space. With this arrangement the listeners are all in touch and the speaker does not feel isolated.

g) Use your equipment and visual aids in conjunction with your speech; don't just leave them as a decorative background to mention after your talk. In fact, a listening group can be 'caught' quickly by holding some interesting object in such a way that they focus their attention.

Photograph taken during an ESB personal project assessment

h) The politest audiences in the world have a tendency to go to sleep or be distracted, so keep them constantly *curious* to know what you are going to tell or show them next.

i) Try to make your group listen *actively*. For example, instead of making a flat statement: 'Jupiter is the largest planet in the solar system', you could present this as a question. 'Which planet, apart from the Sun, is the largest in the solar system?' If there is no reply, *you* supply the answer. When no answer is expected we call it a rhetorical question. (Politicians use this kind of technique: 'And what have the Conservatives (Labour, SDP, Liberals) done in these last three years?' The answers are often as evasive as the questions but it is their way of getting the listeners on their side and holding their attention.)

j) Plan out your talk so that you know what you *want* to include in the time allotted to you, but if one section needs more expansion, indicate that you could enlarge on this in the question time.

k) Don't rush! Material which you gathered together and selected for a two-minute talk will probably need three or four minutes – and so on. If it takes you three minutes to read your talk it will take five minutes to share it with your intelligent listeners!

l)   There are a few ways to overcome nervousness; the main thing is to *enjoy* your subject and enjoy your *listeners*. If you become thoroughly absorbed in both you will forget yourself. This is your privilege and opportunity to communicate some skill or research with personal authority and enthusiasm.

4 Answering questions

Keep your eyes open for the more diffident members of your audience with a hand half-up and then withdrawn. Don't let an assertive person hog the questions. Very often a demonstration accompanying explanation is more graphic than just a verbal reply.

Examples of projects presented by 15/16 year olds in different parts of the UK

The first set are individual talks within a combined group project stemming from a central theme. The letters A, B, C, etc., represent the individual contributions given orally to the listening group. These sections could be done by pairs of speakers.

'OUR TOWN'   Combined group project made up of individual subjects often using films, slides, graphs, maps, diagrams, enlarged photographs and posters.

A   Our town 100 years ago. (A large plan accompanied this talk.)
B   The rock, soil and estuary on which we stand. (Graphic diagrams in bold black felt on white card.)
C   Our river earning its keep. (Pictures of docks and boats.)
D   When and how the canal was constructed. (Map, diagram and photograph.)
E   Our major industries. (Posters had been lent by three major firms.)
F   Our local government. (A chart showing the jobs in a 'tree'.)
G   Where the rates go. (Graphic symbolic division of a £ and a chart showing rate growth.)
H   The art gallery and museum. (Programmes and posters.)
I   Looking after the old people in our town. (Statistics chart and photographs of young helpers.)
J   Our transport system. (Chart showing change from trams to buses and 'pay-as-you-enter' system.)
K   Traffic problems. (Map of crucial points and the intended bypass.)
L   Education in our town. (Distribution of school and student population chart.)
M   Parks, cemeteries and cleansing. (Projected transparencies of the parks, cemeteries and sewers.)

N   Our hospital services. (Photographs and short film.)
O   Future plans. (Motorway, Leisure Centre plans.)

(See other possible group themes at the end of this chapter.)

Individual project talks presented for actual oral assessment in 5th and 6th forms

1   Keeping an aquarium. (Transparencies projected.)
2   My aviary. (Diagrams and bird in cage.)
3   Bee-keeping. (Bee-keeper's equipment, specimens of honey, diagrams of bee 'patterns' and 'dances'.)

Personal project: acupuncture

4 Bread-making with organic stone-ground flour. (Completed loaf brought, process demonstrated with cooking utensils.)

5 Collecting and repairing clocks. (A family hobby. One or two specimen diagrams and photographs.)

6 Climbing. (Equipment worn, large diagrams, photographs.)

7 Dress designing or making. (Different stages completed, material, patterns, technique demonstrated.)

8 Deep-sea diving. (Equipment worn, diagrams, underwater photographs.)

9 How to use an electric drill. (Drill and different components, demonstration of use.)

10 Replacing a part in a car engine. (Diagrams and worn parts handled and shown.)

11 Training a pony (Grooming and saddlery equipment.)

12 Many different talks on aspects of farming – milking machines, combine harvesters, turkey farming, sheep pests, pig diseases, etc. (Films, transparencies, diagrams, graphs, costing charts, etc.)

13 How the Giro works. (Charts, diagrams, records, costings.)

14 The future of Britain's natural gas industry. (Diagrams, enlarged photographs, charts, graphs.)

15 Heraldry. (Charts, diagrams, generation 'collage' built up during talk.)

16 Heart transplants (Plastic model of heart, anatomical drawings, charts, authentic photographs.)

17 Irrigating Lincolnshire farmland. (Aerial film, diagrams, charts.)

18 Intensive poultry farming. (Diagrams, photographs, charts, laying statistics, etc.)

19 Judo. (Costume worn by speaker, demonstration of techniques with partner, drawings.)

20 The extraction of jewels from Kimberlite. (Diagrams, charts, maps.)

21 Making a kaleidoscope. (Different stages shown with mathematical drawings, drawing of design presentations.)

22 Use and care of a food mixer. (Apparatus demonstrated with various food samples.)

23 Designing and making an electric lamp stand in stainless steel. (Finished model, technical drawing of mathematical design, hacksaw, drill, etc.)

24 Pillow lace-making. (Lace bobbins, designs, pillow demonstration.)

25 Macramé work. (Many samples, demonstration of knotting, 'teaching of group'.)

26 Employment at Marks and Spencers. (Personnel charts, instructions, rules for goods on counter, social services, etc.)

27 The making of a local newspaper. (Samples of metals, layout, photographs, charts showing personnel time schedules.)

28 The future of nuclear power. (Aerial photographs of nuclear power stations, physics formulae on charts, etc.)

Demonstration and talk on fell walking

29 Ostrich farming on the Spey. (Samples of feathers, maps, diagrams, photographs.)

30 Tests on motor oils. (Demonstrations, comparative graphs.)

31 Making models from polystyrene. (Examples of masks, mobiles and mathematical 'solids'.)

32 Helping with offset-litho printing. (Commercial leaflets of the machine, metal and paper plates, finished samples.)

33 Quality and quantity. (Tests done on packets of detergent, samples, packets and charts.)

34 Lighting plot for production of *Oliver*. (Plot, chart, control-board diagram – acting areas, etc.)

35 Holiday job in an old people's rest home. (Plan of house, timetable of duties of staff.)

36 The use and care of an electric sewing machine. (Model demonstrated.)

37 Making a sand-yacht. (Plans, drawings, photographs – sand-yacht itself could be seen from window.)

38 Work in a timber-yard. (Pictures and diagrams with words in action with tools during demonstration.)

39 Traditional jazz. (Short extracts on tape with commentary, speaker playing own guitar.)

40 Upholstering a chair. (Model brought, samples of various stages and drawings.)

41 Ultimate. (Speculative account of 'Future Shock', where world is heading, this included the speaker's own poetry which was read during the talk.)

42 Vandalism. (Statistics of damage, cost of restoring, types of culprits, punishment, education.)

43 Vegetarian cookery. (Samples of food, wholemeal flour, raw sugar, etc., protein statistics of cereals on large chart.)

44 Wrought iron work. (Drawing of smithy forge, bellows, tools brought and demonstrated.)

45 Weaving. (Drawings of early looms, photographs of modern electric loom, explanation of processes.)

46 X-rays. (X-ray photographs shown and 'read'.)

47 Making a xylophone. (Mathematically correct proportions of metal pieces to produce the precise note, finished model.)

48 Enzyme action of yeast. (Samples, demonstration, baking, brewing, etc.)

A dressmaking project assessed by the teacher and external examiners

49   Making of yoghourt. (Apparatus brought, sample cartons of commercial yoghourt, comparative costs.)

50   The signs of the Zodiac and their symbolism. (Large charts with signs and dates.)

51   Zip-fasteners. (Inventor, enlarged diagram of 'teeth', samples, ideas drawn for next phase.)

52   Experiences as a 'young volunteer'. (Handouts showing how a volunteer enumerates skills etc., instruction sheets for work undertaken.)

53   Life in a work camp. (Diagrams, charts, photographs showing young people working with skilled artisans.)

54   Gadgets made for the disabled. (Examples brought, designs and drawings of others.)

55   A visit to Martin Mere and the follow-up work in ornithology and conservation. (Maps, diagrams, handout leaflets.)

56   Learning from 'digging' at a Roman settlement in Northumbria. (Charts, diagrams, specimens.)

Many of the subjects listed above could be extended to 'paired' talk or group projects.

Making your own assessment

Copy out this table in your books, one for each speaker. Put a tick in one of the five squares, e.g. if speech is clear and strong, put a tick in 5; if difficult to hear in 1, 2 or 3. There is no question of being right or wrong; it is a means whereby you can give help and encouragement to one another. Be particularly helpful and generous. Give praise where praise is due and constructive criticism on weaknesses.

Name _____ Project _____

		1	2	3	4	5
Voice and speech	clear, strong speech					
Visual aids	well arranged subject matter					
Presentation	lively presentation					
Content & marshalling of facts	well informed					
Answering of questions	informative courteous helpful					

STAGE 2   Group projects

1 Choosing a theme

In Mode 3 of the English Speaking Board senior examinations a group of five to eight candidates may work together on a composite theme.

This productive activity takes place, of course, in many schools and colleges (ideally where there is team-teaching) stemming from the English, drama, or social studies classes.

Demonstrating the skill of rowing using lacrosse sticks

Great adventure and ingenuity go into the search for appropriate material which can be drawn from factual documents, poetry, anthologies, novels, plays, newspapers and magazines. These spoken extracts, quotations and recitals should be linked together with your own commentary. Grouping should be significant and supple, moving subtly into new shapes as the mood and content change. Recorded, or better still, live music, song and group-speaking can be woven into the theme and, possibly, dance-drama.

Examples of themes, witnessed by the authors, carried out by groups in school and technical colleges:

War
Love
Beliefs & doubts
Music
The spirit of
    Christmas presents
The six-pointed star
The four seasons
    (one or four groups)
Seven ages of Man
Monsters
'Sea-change' – a look
    into the future to life
    on the ocean bed
The Common and Uncommon Market
The future
Sound
Space
Ambition
Marriage
Hunger
Hands
Heaven & Hell
Happiness
Prejudice
Time
Damaged lives
Energy
Crabbed age & youth
The modern Samaritan
Good food
Education
The Zodiac
The price of coal
Modes and manners
The Willow pattern plate
Our town
Fashion
Non-tourist London

2 Making a record

In rehearsal use a tape-recorder for personal and critical group listening; finally, when your project has 'jelled' and is good enough for other listeners, record again carefully, making sure that this is carried out at a time when extraneous noise is minimal.

If your recording is a success, you could give pleasure to other groups and classes by lending the tape and perhaps start a borrowing exchange of tapes with other classes or other schools. Satisfactory production of such a theme takes *time*. Be prepared to use out-of-school time in your research for worthwhile material and subsequent rehearsal.

Personal project: 'running the bar'

Some of the most memorable group projects have been about surprising subjects . . .

a) Running a school pre-school play group (the author visited this and met helpers and mothers.)
b) A rota of 'readers' for the local blind people's home.

c) Keeping weather records (these were checked with the local meteorological office and were accepted by them).

d) Running our class 'stock exchange' (the allotted 'money' was a mythical figure from which investments were made from studying the *Financial Times*.)

e) 'For God's sake ...' (this was a composite presentation which included students who were: Roman Catholic; Protestant; Salvation Army; Moslem; Mormon; Buddhist, etc. showing their basic beliefs but how they varied in detail of dogma).

f) School caféteria (this included questionnaires showing which foods were chosen; exposition of junk or sugary foods.)

g) Marriage (this included personal comments; judgements on attitudes of men and women; ex-marital relationships; divorce and birth statistics; legal status, etc.; non-married partnerships; in addition to the factual reports the programme included extracts from novels, plays and poetry.)

h) 'When I am eighteen ...' (this ranged through social, work, legal, and personal aspects of 'coming of age' together with ambitions and aspirations. It included quotations from novels, poems and newspaper articles.)

i) 'We've given up smoking' (this was a group of six students who took the health and financial aspects. It also included the government's income and the advertisers' role.)

j) 'Meals on Wheels' (this was an account given by three boys and three girls on their experiences in helping with meals and the different personalities they encountered).

k) 'Live-Aid' (a report of a show put on by the speakers to make money for African famine).

l) 'Producing a school newspaper' (different editions were on display and the processes of getting copy, editing, illustrating, printing, etc., were given with details of timing and costing).

8 Dialogue in action

'Making a drama out of it', 'Acting tough', 'She's a bit of an actress' – many people associate drama with showing off, pretending and self-indulgence. By 16, most students have usually decided that acting is not for them or that it's a great way of expressing themselves – a few people may be prepared to act out a scene, awkwardly, to help with an English exam but they have fairly fixed ideas on what they can bring to it. So, if you're a keen actor or actress, you may find the exercises below familiar – in places; they will, however, test you in many different ways and not all of them will be what you expect. If you're anti-drama, you may find that these situations aren't as far-fetched and make-believe as you anticipate; we all act, to some extent, as we can't and shouldn't always reveal exactly what we feel and think, if we hope that other people will treat us considerately. If you're not strongly interested or repelled when someone talks about drama, it's worth practising some of the skills it demands; interviews, exam orals, meetings with just about anybody except your closest friends require some stage-management, careful delivery of lines and precise movements – not to pretend you're someone you aren't, but to concentrate your audience's attention on the parts of you that you particularly want them to understand.

The school play may have prestige, but regular drama sessions, which probably produce far more varied and original results, are often seen as excuses for noise, uncontrolled excess and 'mucking around'. Drama is exciting because it does go out of the teacher's hands, into your hands. You don't need anything more than a clear space, a clear set of guidelines and a willingness to move and speak beyond what school normally demands – a sort of passive obedience. That doesn't mean active disobedience immediately takes over, but a co-operative exploration.

1 Simulations

A safe way to start exploring, using a clear map, is to play a role which is clearly laid down for you. Many charity organisations produce games to illustrate a theme – council decisions on housing (Shelter), government decisions on arms spending (Campaign against the Arms Trade), international distribution of resources (Oxfam). You are given details of the character you must play and their attitude to controversial issues.

Greenham District Council

Councillor Ted Briggs
Chairman of the Council

Last year you retired from the secondary school where you taught for 40 years, ending up as assistant headmaster. The children thought you were strict but a good teacher.

You are the only person on the council who has lived in Greenham all his life and for this reason you feel you know better than anyone else what is right for the town. You are very pleased at the way Greenham is growing and take pride in the fact that it was you who first persuaded the director of the chemical plant to bring his factory to the town.

Now you particularly want to encourage anything which would give a boost to industry (for example the new by-pass) or trade (for example the proposed shopping centre). In your youth you were a keen swimmer and cricketer and so you always champion the sporting facilities of the town. You still play golf, usually with your good friend Councillor Geoffrey Worth, the director of the chemical works.

You are not married and the reputation of Greenham is more important to you than anything else in your life. You get very angry when the town is criticised.

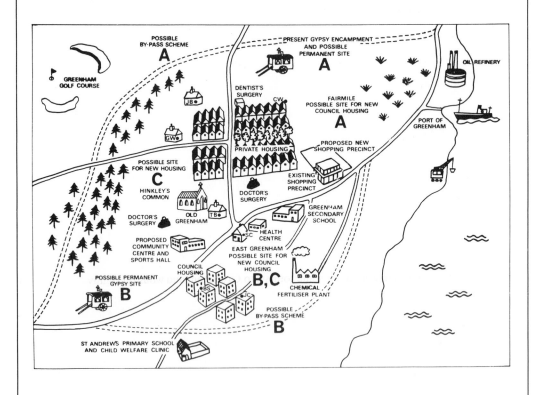

An example of the choices that characters have to make, in role, for the simulation of Greenham District Council's meeting.

ITEM 4

The sports and community complex

Briefing from the Borough Engineer's and Recreation Departments.

Problems

a) Young adults in Greenham have the pubs and the twice weekly bingo hall to choose between if they want a night out.

b) The nearest large town is Skelthorpe, twenty miles away but the last bus leaves for Greenham at 9 p.m.

c) There is no disco in the town and any visiting groups play in an ugly wooden hut which was built forty years ago when Greenham was a village.

d) Apart from a couple of football pitches and the golf club there are no sporting facilities worth talking about in Greenham.

e) There is no swimming pool within twenty miles of Greenham.

f) There has been a great deal of vandalism particularly on the council estate, where windows have been broken and telephone boxes wrecked.
Many people say that if the young had something more interesting to do at night they would not go around beating Greenham up.

g) Young people in particular complain that they are bored in Greenham.

Possible solution

A sports hall, community centre and swimming pool would go a long way towards meeting Greenham's need for leisure facilities. It is possible however that we may not be able to afford all three in the immediate future.

Sports hall

This would be for five-a-side football, basketball, netball, indoor cricket, badminton. It would have spectator facilities as well and would cost £130,000.

Swimming pool

There are two choices here. We could build an indoor heated pool, 50 metres in length which would be large enough for local swimming tournaments and which would cost £140,000. Or, and this proposal has some support locally, we could build a pool of olympic width which might attract some tourists to Greenham and would certainly make the town well known outside. The olympic-size pool would cost an extra £50,000.

Community centre

This would have a bar, coffee-bars, a dance hall/meeting hall/theatre and a number of small rooms for meetings of local clubs and associations. It would cost £130,000.

Costs: Sports hall £130,000; Community centre £130,000; Swimming pool £140,000 (olympic size £190,000).

An example from 'Greenham District Council', a simulation of a Council meeting with seven items on the agenda and limited finance, that has to be split according to the characters' priorities: 'Ted Briggs – Chairman. Retired teacher. Born and bred in Greenham, and extremely keen to encourage industry. Enthusiastic sportsman. Friend of Geoffrey Worth.' 'Geoffrey Worth. Managing Director of chemical plant. Thinks council spending should be as little as possible . . .' Immediately, you are given signs of vested interests, likely allies, likely enemies and enough background material to build a character and confront other people with his strong feelings.

At the end of every simulation, it is important to have a debriefing session in which you can reflect on what 'your' character said and did. You may be surprised how easily you become a bigot, a power-crazy nation or a competitive exploiter and it is worth examining what pressures or temptations bring out such successful acting.

2 Role playing

If you find that you can fill out the roles given you in a simulation, you may want to move on and write your own part – either by creating a similar set of problems and participants as some of the games you've played or by inventing a full character who can enter into any situation and react convincingly. Obviously, this is very ambitious. Mike Leigh, the professional theatre director who has pioneered this sort of extensive improvisation for plays like *Abigail's Party* and *Goose Pimples*, works with his actors for weeks before devising a story and, ultimately, a script. The actors live, work and breathe the character's life they have started to build up – for instance, they may spend a whole day, in the part, dressing, shopping, meeting friends and working. This is quite beyond the scope of a weekly drama lesson or even a group project, but the same principles can apply to creating a character.

a) Think of the person you want to portray. This should, preferably, be a person you've seen and know a little about, but you're not aiming to mimic them – apart from embarrassing them you would be just concentrating on mannerisms and not putting yourself into a character from the inside. Once you've decided on the person (who could be from literature or TV or any medium, provided they're deep enough to explore), walk round the room as you imagine they would.

b) Start to react to the surroundings as they would. Either look at the school buildings or view from the window in character, or, if you find this more helpful, imagine yourself into a setting that the character would normally occupy. This should not be too exotic – the more you get away from your own experience, the less convincing the portrayal. So, if you must act a film star, show them coming home tired after a hard day's work or having trouble doing their homework or learning lines, rather than attending a lavish party (unless you know all about the various ways lavish parties are run).

c) Start to talk as your character would. Discuss what you see with an imaginary friend or enemy. Phone them. Write them a letter – aloud. Don't worry what everyone else is thinking of this impression – they should all be acting out their character's feelings.

d) By now you should have started to show a consistent person who is clearly not you. You've talked and walked like them. Now sit down as you think they would (carelessly, awkwardly, painfully, fussily etc.) and think about their day. Do they get up early? How do they feel as they get up? Do they live on their own? Do they have a large breakfast, a small one or none at all? Why? Are they in a hurry to get out, or indifferent? If your answer starts to be 'How do I know?', make it up. A group leader can take you through some of these questions, while you sit concentrating on the answers.

e) Hot-seating. The hardest and most interesting stage. Put each member of the group, in turn, into a central seat. All the others (in their real characters, not in their assumed ones) cross-examine one of the group, who is in character: what's his or her ambition? how old is he? how successful has his life been? does he have any regrets? There's no limit to the questions that really nosey interviewers can dream up and the embarrassment is contained by the role, not, we hope, felt by the interviewee. He or she must answer, in the way that the character would (angrily, thoughtfully, distantly, expansively . . .). Then, when all the group have taken the hot seat, discuss whose responses were most surprising, and well-sustained. This should reveal all sorts of psychological insights and, quite incidentally, good acting.

3 Script – everyday problems

Working from a good writer's script is an excellent way of practising good speech; you know the words were meant to be spoken, unlike some memorable literary writing; you can rely on the scene to have a variety and shape that an extract from a prose work may lack; you can incorporate good dialogue into many of the exercises prescribed by exam boards – you don't have to hope that material you've created will work in a group project, you know that a succssful scene, well cast and powerfully and intelligently delivered, has impressed many audiences already. You have to find the tempo, tone and understanding that will release the power of the script.

This first extract takes a familiar situation: a husband and wife having a cup of tea after dinner. This trivial, regular ritual reveals all sorts of irritations and frustrations: Alan Ayckbourn, the author, has used a neat device to show the audience how badly communications have broken down. The lines in italics are addressed to each other, but the characters' real thoughts are in normal type and addressed to the audience. So there is a great deal of careful timing and projection needed to convey these normally unspoken thoughts: they come out more funnily and shockingly, because the person they're discussing is a few feet away, oblivious of the enormous irritation the speaker feels – and then voicing new irritations on their own behalf.

The husband is reading the evening paper to himself, but has started to laugh at something he's reading – a sure sign that he will bore his wife still further with a discussion of an article or joke in the paper. The husband is already feeling superior because he's proved how incompetent his wife is, by finding the whistle from the kettle in the sugar bowl – they're both tired of each other and their totally predictable evenings together, but they keep up a pretence of chatter; the husband is particularly concerned about the right and wrong way to keep the boiler working properly, but first he talks to the audience about how he'll intrigue his wife, laughing over the newspaper article.

HUSBAND: This laugh'll keep her in suspense. She's dying to know what it is. Well let her wait . . . (HE LAUGHS AGAIN.)

WIFE: I know. (SHE LAUGHS SUDDENLY.)

HUSBAND: What's she laughing at? She's waiting for me to ask, isn't she? Well, I'm not going to.

WIFE: I must try and keep my eyes open.

HUSBAND: Man here pushed his wife under a bus. I'll make sure she reads that.

WIFE: Why's my husband such an old man? He's always been old. When he was young he was old.

THE HUSBAND FOLDS HIS NEWSPAPER.

Oh no . . . I know what that means . . .

HUSBAND: Oh well, here we go . . . conversation time. *How's the boiler been today?*

WIFE: If he tells me I choked up the air vent with coke, I shall bring a shovel full . . . right into this room, and I shall . . . *No trouble at all today.*

HUSBAND: *Good, must have learnt to behave itself at last, eh?* (HE CHUCKLES).

SHE LAUGHS.

Oh very funny. Ought to be on the music halls I should.

WIFE: What a man. Not only does he make the worst jokes I've ever heard, he makes the same ones . . .

HUSBAND: *You see, if you keep the air vent unclogged, you're all right.*

WIFE: *So it said in the instructions.*

HUSBAND: I thought we'd get back to that. She's flinging that book of instructions in my face again. I tell her something I know for a fact and what does she do . . . take my word for it? Not on your life.

WIFE: When did I last laugh? I mean really laugh? I do believe it was at our wedding reception . . . Something he must have said. What did he say? What could he have said . . . how did he make me laugh?

HUSBAND: That cycling tour we had. What a good time that was. Rained every day too. We didn't care . . . We had some laughs. That's what it was, she used to laugh a lot.

WIFE: *The instruction book also says that we shouldn't overfill it with coke . . . either. That might have been the trouble.*

HUSBAND: *Possibly.* She's got coke on the brain . . . that woman. Looks like a bit of coke. Dehydrated. All the goodness sucked out of her. Supposing I . . . supposing I was to make her laugh. Would it help? Tell her a joke, if only she'd smile properly I think I could almost put up with her. Oh, that miserable face. If only I could make her laugh.

WIFE: He's looking very animated this evening. It's finding that whistle. One little thing like that to hold over me just makes his evening. And when I spilt tea on the new table the other morning, he was so delighted. What did he say? 'Trust you'. As though I went round regularly pouring scalding tea on the veneer.

HUSBAND: *That little business of the sugar basin . . . reminds me . . . of something rather amusing . . . a little story . . .*

WIFE: Hello, what's he up to . . . a little story? He's certainly rubbing it in isn't he? *What's that, dear?*

HUSBAND: *It's nothing really . . . rather silly . . .*

WIFE: Bound to be.

HUSBAND: I've done it now. I'm up to my neck in it. What on earth made me do this? I must be mad.

WIFE: *What is it?* Let's get it over with.

HUSBAND: *It's about two people in a café . . . and one of them is talking about people's funny habits, you see . . . he's saying that everyone is slightly odd in some way or other . . . You see . . . And this other chap says 'not everyone at all. I've nothing peculiar about me. I'm completely normal you see.'*

WIFE: Oh, I can see where this is going.

HUSBAND: *Anyway this first bloke says 'oh no, you're as bad as the rest'. And the other bloke says 'how'?*

WIFE: Or do I think he's just telling me a joke. Why's he doing this.

HUSBAND: *Are you listening?*

WIFE: *Yes dear?*

HUSBAND: *So the bloke says, 'Well now, I've just observed that you just stirred your tea with your right hand . . . '*

WIFE: Why do people tell jokes? To make other people laugh. Why does he want to make me laugh? Does he really want to make me laugh? He must do. It's the only explanation. He *wants* me to laugh.

HUSBAND: *'Yes,' said the bloke. 'Well, that's your peculiarity' said the other bloke. 'Most people use a spoon.'*

WIFE: Just like he used to. He used to walk me home and father said we were peculiar because we just used to stand outside and laugh . . . well most of the time . . . and then we married, and . . . and now it's amazing . . . I think he really wants to . . . he wants to. *Yes, dear, go on, I'm listening.*

HUSBAND: *I've finished.*

WIFE: *Oh.*

HUSBAND: *Not really very funny. I think I'll just take a look at that boiler . . . just to make sure.* (HE EXITS.)

WIFE: (SLOWLY). *You'll find the instructions on the window ledge.*

THE LIGHTS ON THE CENTRAL ACTING AREA FADE TO BLACKOUT AS THE SOUNDS OF VICTOR SYLVESTER ARE HEARD ONCE MORE.

Alan Ayckbourn, *Countdown*

1 Imagine you're directing this piece. What instructions would you give to the actress playing the wife . . .

a) when she laughs?
b) when she changes from speaking to the audience, to addressing her husband, in the same speech?
c) for her speeches of three lines or more, so they are varied and interesting to listen to?
d) in general: how much do you think she still cares about what her husband thinks and says?

2 Now suggest points for the actor playing the husband:

a) which lines are particularly bitter?
b) which lines are more regretful?
c) where do the husband's emotions change, so that he will have to speak with a different intensity or at a different speed?

3 Now do the scene in two ways: once as a very aggressive scene in which the marriage is definitely on the rocks – this is the final break-up; and once as a more resigned scene, which has happened, in more or less the same way, many times, and will happen again. Which interpretation works better and why?

4 Do you think the romantic band music at the end is a good way to finish?

5 Why is the scene called 'Countdown'?

4 Improvisation

Opening lines

Many situations in real life put you on the spot. You have to react very fast – in an interview, in an exam, in an unexpected meeting, nobody hands you the script.

If you can be flexible in your acting, you can probably be more resourceful in everyday situations.

■ *EXERCISE*

2 × 5 minutes: split the group into two smaller groups, A and B

a) Group A leave the room and wait outside to be called in.

b) Group B are given an opening line to deliver when Group A return.

c) Group A come back and pair off with members of Group B, who now say the lines:

   e.g. Excuse me, St Peter, are you sure I'm dead?
   Do you know what she dared to say to me?
   Why are you selling pork pies that are eight years old?
   Excuse me, can you help me? I'm so lonely.
   My car's broken down and I have to come in and use your 'phone.

   (The essence of all these lines is that they suggest a situation and character briefly: the partner in Group B must react – 'No' or 'So what?' isn't enough. Who develops the situation will depend on the resourcefulness of the speakers.)

d) Now reverse the situation and send members of Group A out: Group B now have the opening line.

e) The most effective improvisations can then be heard, for no more than a minute by the rest of the group.

Hotter seats

Another way to test a person's articulate ingenuity is for a group to agree to a story about him or her, which they will then impose on the victim; in other words, the victim will be in the hot seat, as for the role-playing exercise, but all the details will be supplied by the interrogators.

■ *EXERCISE*

5-minute sequences for groups of four or five and one interviewee

a) Send the interviewee out of the room, with instructions to come back in two minutes.

b) The group of four or five interviewers must now quickly agree a story which they are going to put to the interviewee. This could be a ludicrous one.

e.g. Why were you climbing up a lamp-post at 12 o'clock last night singing the National Anthem wearing a bear suit?

c) Then call the interviewee in and ask him or her to answer this charge. The interviewee could then claim that this was a sponsored lamp-post climb to raise money for wild-life preservation; that they were training for a mountainering expedition to restore British prestige; that they have suffered a total loss of memory but assume that their everyday job of street-lamp maintenance means such a lot to them that even on the coldest night, they will go out and patriotically mend any broken lights.

d) The interviewers then have to take up the details, to prove them inconsistent or unjustified by previous parts of the interviewee's story. At no point is the interviewee allowed to deny what is put to him or her, though the group of interviewers must, in turn, keep their accusations consistent, however far-fetched. In other words, if one interviewer says, 'Why were your hands covered in blood?' the next one can't say, 'Why were you wearing spotless white gloves?'

By attributing other scenarios to the interviewee, a sinister picture can emerge, as in Kafka's stories. Here are a few opening suggestions:

Why are you wearing a stolen jacket?
Why have you changed the colour of your hair?
Why were you seen yesterday morning trying to drive away a neighbour's car?
Why did you refuse to appear on the television investigation into alcoholism?
Why are you a member of a subversive organisation?
Why do you spend all your money on toasted teacakes?

High and low status

In his excellent book on improvisation called *Impro*, Keith Johnstone points out (in much greater detail than we have space for) that many people are embarrassed to invent new situations or characters, because they feel these are silly or undermining their own identity. This may be a barrier that many people have to overcome in oral English tests, or oral confrontations generally. Johnstone suggests that you overcome your inhibitions by imagining a new status:

HIGH – you are superior, invincible, confident in your open movements and relaxed manner: other people must move out of the way and will always defer to you.

LOW – you are inferior, vulnerable, diffident, closed in your movements and tense: everyone is going to shout at you and tell you to get out of the way. Move from one status to the other and you start to develop real control and confidence.

Good situations to try out these low- and high-status voices and movements:

Entering a classroom – as if you own it/as if everying is dangerous and menacing.

Going into an interview – as if you are bound to get the job/as if you're the last person who could possibly be considered. If the interviewer also plays a high- or low-status character, the combination can be fascinating: how does a low-status interviewee react to a low-status interviewer? How do two high-status interviewers outdo each other?

Getting the sack – a nervous boss may have major problems in breaking the news to a confident employee. Improvising this situation, with a normally quiet person playing the employee, and a normally forceful person playing the boss can develop self-awareness.

Fighting the object – technology or even basic machines like bicycles and washing machines can reduce people to panic: a scene with a low-status victim trying to cope with difficult machinery (if suitable, played by high-status actors) can again show a variety of ways that voice and movement convey authority or insecurity.

Overall, high-status exercises can build up confidence in people who may have little experience of being in a superior or authoritative position. The fact that they can switch between confidence and panic, in an acting situation, can help reverse the process, when they find themselves under pressure and full of low-status fears and anxieties.

5 Script – once-in-a-lifetime problems

In this extract from Jean Anouilh's *Antigone*, Antigone has been sentenced to death for disobeying a state order and burying her rebel brother. As she waits in the condemned cell, her proud certainty starts to crack. She wants to talk to the guard as a human being, but he can only repeat the bloodthirsty order for execution mechanically, after discussing his promotion prospects. In the end, he's prepared to help her, for a price; she dictates a passionate letter to her fiancé, admitting she doesn't know any more why she's a martyr. Antigone's desperate need to explain herself in this last message is a complete contrast to the guard's automatic writing – once again, he's quite content and unquestioning, because somebody is giving him orders.

Antigone

ANTIGONE: Was it you that arrested me this morning?

GUARD: Yes, that was me.

ANTIGONE: You hurt me. There was no need for you to hurt me. Did I act as if I was trying to escape?

GUARD: Come on now, Miss. It was my business to bring you in. I did it. (*A pause. He paces to and fro upstage. Only the sound of his boots is heard.*)

ANTIGONE: How old are you?

GUARD: Thirty-nine.

ANTIGONE: Have you any children?

GUARD: Yes. Two.

ANTIGONE: Do you love your children?

GUARD: What's that got to do with you? (*A pause. He paces upstage and downstage*)

ANTIGONE: How long have you been in the Guard?

GUARD: Since the war. I was in the army. Sergeant. Then I joined the Guard.

ANTIGONE: Does one have to have been an army sergeant to get into the Guard?

GUARD: Supposed to be. Either that or on special detail. But when they make you a guard, you lose your stripes.

ANTIGONE: (*murmurs*) I see.

GUARD: Yes. Of course, if you're a guard, everybody knows you're something special; they know you're an old N.C.O. Take pay, for instance. When you're a guard you get your pay, and on top of that you get six months' extra pay, to make sure you don't lose anything by not being a sergeant any more. And of course you do better than that. You get a house, coal, rations, extras for the wife and kids. If you've got two kids, like me, you draw better than a sergeant.

ANTIGONE: (*barely audible*). I see.

GUARD: That's why sergeants, now, they don't like guards. Maybe you noticed they try to make out they're better than us? Promotion, that's what it is. In the army, anybody can get promoted. All you need is good conduct. Now in the Guard, it's slow, and you have to know your business – like how to make out a report and the like of that. But when you're an N.C.O. in the Guard, you've got something that even a sergeant-major ain't got. For instance—

ANTIGONE: (*breaking him off*). Listen.

GUARD: Yes, Miss.

ANTIGONE: I'm going to die soon.

The GUARD *looks at her for a moment, then turns and moves away.*

GUARD: For instance, people have a lot of respect for guards, they have. A guard may be a soldier, but he's kind of in the civil service, too.

ANTIGONE: Do you think it hurts to die?

GUARD: How would I know? Of course, if somebody sticks a sabre in your guts and turns it round, it hurts.

ANTIGONE: How are they going to put me to death?

GUARD: Well, I'll tell you. I heard the proclamation all right. Wait a minute. How did it go now? *(He stares into space and recites from memory.)* 'In order that our fair city shall not be pol-luted with her sinful blood, she shall be im-mured – immured.' That means, they shove you in a cave and wall up the cave.

ANTIGONE: Alive?

GUARD: Yes . . . *(He moves away a few steps.)*

ANTIGONE: *(murmurs).* O tomb! O bridal bed! Alone! *(ANTIGONE sits there, a tiny figure in the middle of the stage. You would say she felt a little chilly. She wraps her arms round herself.)*

GUARD: Yes! Outside the south-east gate of the town. In the Cave of Hades. In broad daylight. Some detail, eh, for them that's on the job! First they thought maybe it was a job for the army. Now it looks like it's going to be the Guard. There's an outfit for you! Nothing the Guard can't do. No wonder the army's jealous.

ANTIGONE: A pair of animals.

GUARD: What do you mean, a pair of animals?

ANTIGONE: When the winds blow cold, all they need do is to press close against one another. I am all alone.

GUARD: Is there anything you want? I can send out for it, you know.

ANTIGONE: You are very kind. *(A pause.* ANTIGONE *looks up at the* GUARD.) Yes, there is something I want. I want you to give someone a letter from me, when I am dead.

GUARD: How's that again? A letter?

ANTIGONE: Yes, I want to write a letter; and I want you to give it to someone for me.

GUARD: *(straightens up).* Now, wait a minute. Take it easy. It's as much as my job is worth to go handing out letters from prisoners.

ANTIGONE: *(removes a ring from her finger and holds it out towards him).* I'll give you this ring if you will do it.

GUARD: Is it gold? *(He takes the ring from her.)*

ANTIGONE: Yes, it is gold.

GUARD: *(shakes his head).* Uh-uh. No can do. Suppose they go through my pockets. I might get six months for a thing like that. *(He stares at the ring, then glances off right to make sure that he is not being watched.)* Listen, tell you what I'll do. You tell me what you want to say, and I'll write it down in my book. Then, afterwards, I'll tear out the pages and give them to the party, see? If it's in my handwriting, it's all right.

ANTIGONE: *(winces).* In your handwriting? *(She shudders slightly.)* No. That would be awful. The poor darling! In your handwriting.

GUARD: *(offers back the ring).* O.K. It's no skin off my nose.

ANTIGONE: *(quickly).* Of course, of course. No, keep the ring. But hurry. Time is getting short. Where is your notebook? *(The* GUARD *pockets the ring, takes his notebook and pencil from his pocket, puts his foot up on chair, and rests the notebook on his knee, licks his pencil.)* Ready? *(He nods.)* Write, now. 'My darling . . .'

GUARD: *(writes as he mutters).* The boy friend, eh?

ANTIGONE: 'My darling. I wanted to die, and perhaps you will not love me any more . . .'

GUARD: *(mutters as he writes)* '. . . will not love me any more.'

ANTIGONE: 'Creon was right. It is terrible to die.'

GUARD: *(repeats as he writes)* '. . . terrible to die.'

ANTIGONE: 'And I don't even know what I am dying for. I am afraid . . .'

GUARD: *(looks at her)*. Wait a minute! How fast do you think I can write?

ANTIGONE: *(takes hold of herself)*. Where are you?

GUARD: *(reads from his notebook)*. 'And I don't even know what I am dying for.'

ANTIGONE: No. Scratch that out. Nobody must know that. They have no right to know. It's as if they saw me naked and touched me, after I was dead. Scratch it all out. Just write: 'Forgive me.'

GUARD: *(looks at* ANTIGONE*)*. I cut out everything you said there at the end, and I put down, 'Forgive me'?

ANTIGONE: Yes. 'Forgive me my darling. You would all have been so happy except for Antigone. I love you.'

GUARD: *(finishes the letter)*. '. . . I love you.' *(He looks at her)* Is that all?

ANTIGONE: That's all.

GUARD: *(straightens up, looks at notebook)*. Damn funny letter.

ANTIGONE: I know.

GUARD: *(looks at her)*. Who is it to? *(A sudden roll of drums begins and continues until after* ANTIGONE *exits. The* FIRST GUARD *pockets the notebook and shouts at* ANTIGONE*)* O.K. That's enough of you! Come on.

(At the sound of the drum roll, SECOND *and* THIRD GUARDS *enter through the right arch.* ANTIGONE *rises.* GUARDS *seize her and exit with her.)*

Jean Anouilh, *Antigone*

When dealing with any piece of drama, you need to ask your actors (or yourself, if you're acting a part) several key questions:

Why does a character behave like this? For example, how does the guard feel when he is accused of being too brutal in arresting Antigone? Why does he become so talkative about being a guard – is this pride, relief at changing the subject to an area he knows or an attempt to take Antigone's mind off her misery? Why does he disobey orders and agree to write a message – is it pure greed or sympathy for Antigone? Does he care for her or understand her better at the end than at the start?

When Antigone 'murmurs' and is 'barely audible', why is she so quiet? Do you think she's self-pitying as she realises what faces her? Why does she change her message to 'Forgive me'? Does she feel she has achieved something by the end of the scene – this will greatly affect how she says her last two speeches, for which Anouilh gives no directions – 'That's all' and 'I know'.

How does a character time a speech? Look carefully at the instructions to pause and to move. This will reflect uncertainty, embarrassment, tension and many other emotions which should come out in the actor's or actress's voice.

For a long speech, there must be pace and variety, otherwise monotony quickly sets in. Look at the two big speeches by the guard about being in the army – decide how he can become more enthusiastic, conceited or confidential, when he's saying these. He has to be sensitively insensitive, since he's very preoccupied by his job and prospects, but quite indifferent – at least on the surface – to what Antigone is feeling. When she 'breaks him off' and says, 'Listen', the conversation becomes much more serious and urgent – does he speak more slowly for the next three speeches? How can you make her very basic and almost stupid questions moving?

How do characters stand and move in relation to each other? Though this is not a book about performing plays, you can apply dramatic techniques to make a series of speeches have more impact. In the section just discussed, the Guard is said to 'look at her for a moment, then turn and move away' and he moves away again at the end of the sequence. Antigone is given no directions – should she follow him, and talk urgently to him, or are her questions more inward or directed at the audience rather than him? They must be audible, but they must also show, by the way she points them (literally and metaphorically) where her emotions and energy are going.

6 Sounds

These exercises would fit as well into the chapter on voice, but because they demand uninhibited delivery of some very odd noises, they come here, after you've practised a wide variety of different drama techniques. Throughout, you should be checking your control of breathing; your posture – is it fully relaxed? (Don't for instance, stand with arms crossed over the area that must expand most – your diaphragm, or sit slumped in a chair.) Are both vowels and consonants fully formed and clear? Is the tone full or, for words that must be said in contrasting ways, emotionally appropriate?

Audibility: say these words at different speeds and volumes:
Himonoosh; mood-maud; myxamotosis; 1-2-3-POW!; Peggy Babcock; Continental fruit mousse.

Variations: say these words to mean at least three different responses:
Yes (e.g. Yes, please, I'd love another sweet; Yes, if I absolutely have to; No); No; Me; You; I don't know; It's all right for some people; You're sorry; Saturday; Never.

Articulation: say these repeatedly, as fast and clearly as possible:
Mixed biscuits; yellow lorry leather, red lorry leather; proper coffee pot; Hugh has hewed down the yew you used to view in youthful years; eyes, nose, cheeky cheeky chin, hands, cheeky cheeky chin, nose, eyes (preferably with finger pointing to the appropriate part).

Sing-song: use chants, plainsong or overinflected delivery for lists of objects – furniture, fruits, countries or animals.

Speaking sounds: lengthen and lighten (or weigh down) words to show their meaning – e.g. balloon, inflate, expand, float, light, break. If these six words are spoken with appropriate actions (e.g. rising as a group from the floor to create a balloon shape) you can rapidly construct a sort of miniature concrete poem.

Backwards: take a well-known sentence or short poem and speak it backwards. This is done to great effect in Sam Sheppard's *Unseen Hand*, where a character speaks 'a strange, ancient language' in a trance.

Reading the register: Rowan Atkinson has a famous sketch where he simply reads out a list of extremely unlikely names, in the spitting, contemptuous voice of a schoolmaster who makes every consonant bounce off the back wall of his classroom: you can devise your own recall, but might like to include some of Atkinson's class – Ainsley, Babcock, Bland, Ditt, Elbourn Beast Major, Elbourn Beast Minor, Kosygin, Nancyboy Potter, Nipple, Orifice, Plectrum, Ta, Undermanager, Zob.

7 Script – film

Though you may not have the facilities to put any of the performances you produce onto video, you can see how professional productions realise a script, if you study the increasing number of transcripts available, before or after watching a film. The extract below takes a familiar situation – bored children on a seaside holiday with their parents – but the script can lead to a great deal of discussion: How should the characters speak and look? What camera shots should be used to bring out their relative importance in the scene? A shot which is taken from the viewpoint of one character immediately puts the viewer into that character's world and sees the other characters from the outside; a shot of one character's face, taken close-up, can be threatening or surprising, if swiftly intercut with other pictures. Read these short scenes then discuss the best way of filming them.

One Fine Day on the Beach

COLIN: I'm bored. *(Pause.)* I'm bored, Dad. *(Pause.)* Dad. I'm bored.

DAD: You're twelve years old.

COLIN: I am.

DAD: It's grown-ups that are bored. You're having the time of your life.

COLIN: I'm bored.

DAD: Well, if you're bored now, you'll be more bored when you're grown up. It gets more boring as you go on.

MAM: You bore me.

COLIN: You bore me.

(DAD clouts him.)

MAM: Jack!

DAD: I don't care. Saying that. We come away on holiday and then he's the cheek to say he's bored.

(COLIN *goes off at this point.*)

MAM: I am getting old arms. My arms. Getting to look right old.

DAD: Why single out your arms?

MAM: Well, I notice you haven't got into your costume.

DAD: Why should I? Who is there to impress?

MAM: Impress! With that belly?

DAD: I impressed you once.

MAM: Ay. you did. You did that. Funny, we've never been to Filey since.

JENNIFER: I'm cold.

MAM: If you say you're cold once more, young lady, I'll think of something to warm you up.

DAD: Come here, love.

(JENNIFER *sits on his knee.*)

MAM: I don't like watching TV in a roomful of folk. *(Pause.)* Do you?

DAD: Do I what?

MAM: Like watching with people you don't know.

DAD: It's all right. *Match of the Day.*

MAM: It's not the same as watching it on our own. I'd rather go to the proper pictures. I hate being sat there with a jorem of folks not knowing what they're like, wondering what they're all thinking. *(Pause.)* Plays. I can't watch plays among strangers. They have to be people I know. Preferably the immediate family. *(Pause.)* You can't talk to it.

DAD: What?

MAM: The TV. I like to talk to it.

DAD: Don't start talking to it up there or they'll think you're barmy.

MAM: Everybody talks to it. Acts daft. If they're on their own, and they think nobody's watching. I do.

DAD: I don't.

(Pause.)

MAM: You're not your own master. Where Dugdales stayed, the Clarendon, that has TV in every bedroom. Shower and TV. 'Private hotel.' It's not a proper private hotel. It's not even that clean. *(Pause.)* That pillow had hairs on it.

DAD: My hairs.

MAM: They weren't your hairs. I know your hairs. I should know your hairs by now. Your hairs aren't like that. They were somebody else's hairs. Little curly ones. I found another one there this morning.

DAD: They won't kill you. The army, we never even had pillowcases. Hairs. *(Pause.)*

MAM: I think it's that that's stopping me sleeping.

DAD: What?

MAM: Them little hairs. I've not had a proper night since we came. Let alone anything else.

DAD: Well, whose fault is that?

MAM: No. I mean the other. At home I always go like clockwork.

DAD: You said the same at Marbella.

MAM: No, I was the other way at Marbella.
DAD: It's the water.
MAM: It's partly the water. But I'm not struck on that toilet. I don't like them low suites.
DAD: Go to one of the other ones.
MAM: It's half a mile. They're like everything else these days, designed for what it looks like. Whereas we're not. We're not designed for what it looks like, are we?
DAD: What?
MAM: Bottoms!
DAD: Lil! I don't know. We come away on holiday and you get right unsavoury. Toilets. Read the paper.

JENNIFER: Dad. Dad.
MAM: Jennifer.
JENNIFER: Dad.
DAD: What?
JENNIFER: Do you like it here?
MAM: Jennifer.
DAD: Why?
JENNIFER: It's cold. The sea's not blue. It's blue abroad.
MAM: I've told you not to talk about abroad. Your father doesn't want to know about abroad. You're lucky to have been abroad. We'd never been abroad at your age. Abroad. We only came on this holiday for you.
DAD: I don't know why we did. When you reckon it all up there's not much difference in price. That place isn't cheap for what you get. And I'm always hungry.
MAM: You pay for him on that radio, that's what you pay for. *(Pause.)* Do you think that couple at the little table are married?
DAD: Not if he's any sense.

> COLIN *wanders down through the people sitting on the sands, out into the bay, trying to walk to the edge of the sea. Miles and miles of empty sand. The beach is very small and distant behind him. The very faint sound of the beach. Finally he reaches the edge of the sea. But he isn't sure whether it really is the edge, it's so gradual and undramatic.*
> *He is called back by shouts of 'Colin!'*

Alan Bennett, *One Fine Day at the Beach*

How does Alan Bennett make this depressing seaside holiday both funny and interesting? Although the few directions in the text suggest that we are seeing it through Colin's eyes, do you think the other characters are treated as sympathetically? How far could some shots work from Mam and Dad's point of view?

At the end of the numbered sequence, what would be the character's expressions that you wanted to show in the closing tableau?

As with other sections in this chapter, the film extract can only whet your appetite for more research and discussion. Film techniques are highly sophisticated and a single page of script may take weeks to set up and turn into a completed minute of screen-time. You can, however, start to think in film terms, e.g. compare the opening of a film or TV dramatisation with the novel it's based on – L. P. Hartley's *The Go-Between* (directed by Joseph Losey) with a screenplay by Harold Pinter, published in Pinter, *Five Screen Plays* (Methuen) is a good start – you can compare the way Pinter has compressed the narrative and created a powerful atmosphere, simply by comparing the two texts, though, obviously, seeing the film is even more of a stimulus.

Other books which are often studied in the fifth and sixth form, with powerful film versions include:

Charles Dickens, *Great Expectations* (David Lean)
       Bleak House (BBC serial)
William Golding, *Lord of the Flies* (Peter Brook)
Barry Hines,   *Kes* (Ken Loach)
Thomas Hardy,   *Tess* (Roman Polanski)
George Orwell,   *Animal Farm* (Halas/Batchelor cartoon)

and many Shakespeare dramatisations, both by the BBC and more large-scale versions – e.g. Zeffirelli's *Romeo and Juliet*, Polanski's *Macbeth*, Olivier's *Othello*.

Work out your own ten opening shots, describing the mood you want to establish for a book you're studying, or any of these topics:

– The town the tourists don't see
– A true ghost story
– Gulliver's new travels
– After the war was over . . .

A few things to check:

1) How near is the Camera? Close-up: camera seems very close to subject; head and shoulders only appear for a human figure; as the camera moves away, think of the effect of a mid-shot (upper half of human figure), full-length shot (showing the whole body) and a wide shot (dwarfing the figure in a landscape).

2) What angle is it at? A low-angle shot, pointing upwards will make a place or person loom ominously; a high-angle shot, pointing down, will diminish them.

3) Whose point of view do you want? Is the scene observed from outside, or do we follow different people's viewpoints, cutting from one to another?

4) How much does the camera move? A pan – swivelling from right to left or left to right; a tracking shot – where the camera follows the action as it moves; a zoom – where the camera moves rapidly into or away from a focus.

5) How does one shot follow another? Does it dissolve, so one image gradually changes into another? Is it 'wiped' so that it is completely and swiftly removed? Is there a 'jump cut' – a jarring change from one shot to the next, often to produce a shock effect? Or is there a 'montage' where one image is superimposed on another? All this can make a valuable exercise in group collaboration, form the basis of talks (with excellent audio-visual material to illustrate them) and build up an appreciation of the way words evoke pictures – every good book appeals to the reader's imagination and this is one way of realising some of the appeal.

8 A complete project

Many of the exercises in this chapter are designed to produce a fairly fast result; many, you can come back to, so that you build up a range of skills over different stages of the course. Time permitting, there's another project which offers great scope for all the skills in this chapter – a full-scale production of Ted Hughes' poetic drama, originally written for radio, *Orpheus*. This incorporates group and individual verse-speaking, imaginative acting and sensitive use of improvisation, sound and light. The music department may be able to provide a live soundtrack to support the script. There is a great deal of powerful, atmospheric music on record, which could be combined to make a memorable soundtrack. There are great challenges to sound and lighting technicians – for instance:

For sound:
What would properly convey the 'storm of cries . . . of all who have died on earth and cannot come back'?

How do you create 'Plutonic laughter in hell' without being corny or ridiculous?

For light:
What are 'appropriate light effects' for someone falling into the kingdom of the dead?

How can the huge proportions of a face 'vast on his vast throne . . . made of black iron' be realised?

There are plenty of challenges for the actors, too. Pluto must convey not only power and menace but helplessness in the face of his silent, unreachable wife. Orpheus must be both maddened by the loss of his own wife and determined, through all the storms of noise and terrors of hell, to strike some bargain with its King.

This final extract demands a great deal from everyone involved in its production, but the finished performance could be both spectacular and moving. There are no further suggestions at the end of the piece, because you are now in charge! This is dialogue for you to direct into vivid action.

(*Orpheus, the master musician, has ignored warnings that his music is dangerous and likely to cost him a terrible price. Suddenly, he finds he cannot play. One of his friends arrives, to bring him appalling news.*)

ORPHEUS: What is your news?

FRIEND: Eurydice is dead.
Magnified crash of strings as if instruments smashed; light effects – sudden darkening.

NARR: Eurydice lies dead in an orchard, bitten by a snake.
Her soul has left her body. Her body is cold.
Her voice has been carried away to the land of the dead.

ORPHEUS: Eurydice!
He lies prostrate. His music – now erratic and discordant – struggles to tormented climax and again collapses as if all instruments smashed. Light effects

NARR: Orpheus mourns for a month and his music is silent.
The trees droop their boughs, they weep leaves.
The stones in the wall weep.
The river runs silent with sorrow under its willows.
The birds sit mourning in silence on the ridge of the house.
Orpheus lies silent and face downwards.

FRIEND: Orpheus, you are mourning too long. The dead are dead.
Remember the living. Let your own music heal your sorrow.
Play for us.

NARR: The trees know better.

TREES: We shall never dance again. Eurydice is dead. Now we return to the ancient sadness of the forest.

NARR: And the stones know better.

STONES: We are the stones, older than life. We have stood by many graves.
We know grief to the bottom. We danced for a while because

Orpheus was happy. Eurydice is dead. Now we return to the
ancient sadness of the hills.

FRIENDS ONE,   Eurydice did not want you to grieve so long, Orpheus.
TWO AND THREE: Play your music again. Deceive your grief. Defeat evil fortunes.
The dead belong to the dead: the living to the living. Play for us.
At last! Orpheus reaches for the magic strings.
One note, repeated, gathering volume and impetus – insane.

FRIENDS ONE,   Horrible! Is this music. He has forgotten how to play. Grief has
TWO AND THREE: damaged his brain. This is not music.

ORPHEUS: I am going down to the underworld. To find Eurydice.

FRIENDS: Mad! He is mad! Orpheus has gone mad!

ORPHEUS: I am going to the bottom of the underworld. I am going to bring
Eurydice back.

FRIEND ONE: Nobody ever came back from the land of the dead.

ORPHEUS: I am going. And I shall come back. With Eurydice.

FRIENDS: Mad! He is mad! Orpheus has gone mad! Nobody ever returns from
the land of the dead.
*Their voices fade. His crazy note strengthens modulating into electronic
infernal accompaniments. Major light effects through what follows.*

NARR: *Speaking with greatly magnified voice over the music – not declaiming
so much as a giant whisper*
Where is the land of the dead? Is it everywhere? Or nowhere?
How deep is the grave?
What is the geography of death?
What are its frontiers?
Perhaps it is a spider's web. Perhaps it is a single grain of dirt.
A million million souls can sit in an atom.
Is that the land of the dead?
A billion billion ghosts in the prison of an atom.
Waiting for eternity to pass.
Orpheus music louder. Light effects.
Orpheus beats his guitar. He is no longer making music. He is making
a road of sound. He is making a road through the sky. A road to
Eurydice.

ORPHEUS: Eurydice! Eurydice! Eurydice!

NARR: He flies on his guitar. His guitar is carrying him. It has lifted him off
the earth. It lifts him over the treetops.
Music continuing, The monotonous note like a drum note insistent.

FRIENDS: Orpheus, come back! Orpheus, come back.

ORPHEUS: Eurydice!

NARR: It carries him into a cloud.
*Light and sound effects through what follows, his music continuing
throughout.*
Through the thunder he flies. Through the lightning.
It carries him
Through the storm of cries
The last cries of all who have died on earth

The jealous, screaming laments
Of all who have died on earth and cannot come back.
Storm of cries.

ORPHEUS: Eurydice!

NARR: He lays his road of sound across the heavens.
His guitar carries him.
Into the storm of blood,
The electrical storm of all the blood of all who have died on earth.
He is whirled into the summit of the storm.
Lightnings strike through him, he falls –

ORPHEUS: Eurydice!

NARR: He falls into the mouth of the earth.
He falls through the throat of the earth, he recovers.

ORPHEUS: He rides his serpent of sound through the belly of the earth.
He drives his spear of sound through the bowels of the earth.
Mountains under the earth fall on him, he dodges.
He flies through walls of burning rock and ashes.
His guitar carries him.
Music continuing monotonous and insane.
He hurtles towards the centremost atom of the earth
He aims his beam of sound at the last atom.

ORPHEUS: Eurydice!

NARR: He smashes through the wall of the last atom.
He falls
He falls
At the feet of Pluto, King of the kingdom of the dead.
Silence, appropriate light effects.

PLUTO: So you have arrived. At first I thought it was a fly. Then I thought it was a meteorite. But now I see – it is a man. A living man, in the land of the dead. Stand. I am Pluto, King of the underworld. And you, I think, are Orpheus.

NARR: Orpheus stands on the floor of the hall of judgement, like a mouse on the floor of a Cathedral. Pluto's face, vast on his vast throne, is made of black iron, and it is the face of a spider. The face of Persephone, his wife and Queen, vast on her vast throne, beside him, is made of white ivory, and it is the pointed, eyeless face of a maggot.

PLUTO: Orpheus! I have heard of you. What is it, Orpheus, brings you alive to the land of the dead?

ORPHEUS: You took away my wife Eurydice.

PLUTO: That is true.

ORPHEUS: What can I do to get her back?

PLUTO: Get her back? *Laughs – Plutonic laughter in hell.*
Alas, your wife has gone into the vaults of the dead. You cannot have her back.

ORPHEUS: Release her. You are a god. You can do as you like.

PLUTO: Some things are not in my power, Orpheus. Here is my wife, for instance, Persephone. Perhaps you have heard about her. Six months she spends with me, here in the underworld. Six months she is up on earth, in the woods and meadows, with her mother. That is the arrangement. Up on the earth she is a flower-face, she laughs and sings, everybody adores her. But now you see her. Here in the underworld she is quite different. She never makes a sound. Never speaks, never sings. And you see her face? It is the peaked face of a maggot. Yet it is not a maggot. It is the white beak of the first sprout of a flower. I have never seen it open. Here in the underworld it is closed: white, pointed and closed: the face of a maggot. Here is something I cannot alter.

There is another thing, Orpheus. Here in the underworld, the accounting is strict. A payment was due from you.

ORPHEUS: Payment.

PLUTO: Nothing is free. Everything has to be paid for. For every profit in one thing – payment in some other thing. For every life – a death. Even your music – of which we have heard so much – that had to be paid for. Your wife was the payment for your music. Hell is now satisfied.

ORPHEUS: You took my wife –

PLUTO: To pay for your music.

ORPHEUS: But I had my music from birth. I was born with it.

PLUTO: You had it on credit. You were living in debt. Now you have paid and the music is yours.

ORPHEUS: Then take back my music. Give me my wife.

PLUTO: Too late.

ORPHEUS: What good is my music without my wife? What can I do to make you give me my wife.

PLUTO: Nothing can open Hell.
Orpheus strikes a chord – no longer pop – solemn Handel, Bach, Vivaldi, or earlier. Light effects.
Music.

PLUTO: Your music is even more marvellous in hell.
Than ever on earth. But it cannot help you.
Music.

ORPHEUS: Look at your wife, Pluto. Look at Persephone, your Queen.
Music.

PLUTO: Her face is opening.

ORPHEUS: A wife for a wife, Pluto. Shall I continue to play?

PLUTO: Keep playing. Keep playing.
Music stops.
Keep playing. Why have you stopped?

ORPHEUS: It is in my power to release the flower
In your wife's face and awake her. Release my wife.

PLUTO: Play.

ORPHEUS: A wife for a wife.

PLUTO: What ever you wish. Only play. You can have your wife.
Music.

PLUTO: Beautiful as the day I plucked her off the earth!
Music stops.

ORPHEUS: You have your wife, Pluto.

PERSEPHONE: Keep your promise, to Orpheus. Give him his wife.

PLUTO: I cannot.

ORPHEUS: Cannot? A god cannot break his promise.
A god's promise is stronger than the god.

PLUTO: I cannot. Your wife's body is crumbling to dust.

PERSEPHONE: Give him her soul.

PLUTO: I can only give you her soul.

ORPHEUS: Let it be so. Let my wife's soul come with me.
Light effects. Dance and mime through what follows.

PLUTO: You who have awakened the Queen of Hell
Return to the world. Your wife's soul will be with you.
Orpheus' new music very soft.

NARR: Orpheus returns to the earth. It is not far. It is only a step.
A step, a step and a step
A step – and he turns. He looks for his wife. The air is empty.
Music stops.

ORPHEUS: Eurydice?

EURYDICE: I am here.

ORPHEUS: Eurydice, where are you? Eurydice?

EURYDICE: Here at your side, Orpheus.

NARR: He cannot see her. He cannot touch her. He can only hear her. He listens.

EURYDICE: Play for me, Orpheus.
Orpheus plays his new music.

NARR: Orpheus' friends come running. They listen to his music. It is no longer the same music.

FRIENDS ONE, TWO AND THREE: This won't make anybody dance.
This is queer music. This is dreary.

FRIEND THREE: Play as you used to play, Orpheus. Make us dance.
Music continues.

NARR: The trees did not dance. But the trees listened.
The music was not the music of dancing
But of growing and withering
Of the root in the earth and the leaf in the light,
The music of birth and of death.

And the stones did not dance. But the stones listened.
The music was not the music of happiness.
But of everlasting, and the wearing away of the hills,
The music of the stillness of stones,
Of stones under frost, and stones under rain, and stones in the sun,
The music of the sea-bed drinking at the stones of the hills.
The music of the floating weight of the earth.
And the bears in their forest-holes
Heard the music of bears in their forest-holes
The music of bones in the starlight

The music of many a valley trodden by bears,
The music of bears listening on the earth for bears.

And the deer on the high hills heard the crying of wolves
And the salmon in the deep pools heard the whisper of the snows
And the traveller on the road
Heard the music of love coming and love going
And love lost forever,
The music of birth and of death.
The music of the earth, swaddled in heaven, kissed by its cloud and
watched by its ray.

And the ears that heard it were also of leaf and of stone. The faces
that listened were flesh of cliff and of river.
The hands that played it were the fingers of snakes and a tangle of
flowers.

Ted Hughes, *Orpheus*

9 Protesting without violence

This chapter deals with three areas where you may want to make a stand and argue strongly to change things – at home, at school or in the community around you. There are ways that you can make an impact without abuse, mindless slogans or personally destructive attacks. 'Personally' refers both to the person you're opposing and to you, since the more fanatical or negative you become in any cause, however good, the lesser person you are. If you get to the point where everything is black and white, simplified and used for only one purpose, you stop learning anything or admitting any possibility of other ways of thinking and that other people are valuable. It may be tempting to shock or undermine people who appear not to hear or understand what you're telling them, but it's more productive to argue with them on their own ground and present rational and dignified alternatives. However long it takes to change their minds, you won't have lost your cause, because you won't have been reduced to a campaign which devalues you or your ideals.

1 Home protest

What are the main issues that cause arguments with your parents?

a) hair-styles
b) clothes
c) staying out late
d) not helping in the house
e) boyfriends/girlfriends
f) friends in general
g) smoking
h) noise

i) television
j) homework
k) quarrelling with brothers/sisters
l) table manners
m) money
n) staying in bed late
o) using the telephone too much
p) using the bathroom or any other room too much

Group discussion

Divide into groups of four or five; choose someone to lead the discussion who hasn't done this before and appoint someone to take notes about what's said.

a) On which points do you differ from your parents?
b) In which ways have you tried to do what they ask?

c) Have they appreciated any efforts you've made to patch up arguments?

d) If they have appreciated your efforts, does this mean you can avoid the next argument? If they haven't responded, why do you think this is?

Discussion about particular topics

This should arise naturally, but if it doesn't, here are a few starting points:

a) & b) **Fashions**: How much right do parents have to criticise or even ban what you wear and how you look? Does the fact that they pay for some of your clothes or provide facilities for you to wash/iron/make them give them any more rights? How far would you criticise what they wear? How would they react to this criticism?

c) **Staying out late**: Is it possible to reach an agreement about a reasonable time to come home? How far should these points affect the time – disturbance and worry to your parents, late at night? The fact that many of your friends can stay out all night? The danger of travelling home late and, possibly, alone? The need to get up and work next day?

d) **Not helping in the house**: How many of these jobs should you be asked to share? Bed-making; washing-up; vacuuming; washing clothes; preparing meals; decorating; gardening; cleaning the car; taking the dog for walks/looking after other pets? Put these in order of importance and compare your list with other people's.

e) & f) **Friends**: If you were in your parents' place, would you want your son and daughter to bring home friends who were noisy, violent, drunk, drug-users, scruffy, smoking, driving cars or motor-bikes recklessly/riding bikes to show off, indifferent to what parents said to them, cheeky, outrageous, strange? How many of these things apply to your friends? Do you find these qualities less important when you're meeting somebody than your parents do? Why?

g) **Smoking**: 'It's my life and I can do what I like with it.' All medical experts now agree: smoking heavily, particularly from an early age, causes severe health problems and probably shortens your life. Each cigarette, it is said, takes five minutes off your life: if you've smoked regularly from the age of ten or eleven, by the time you're sixteen, you'll have spent hundreds of pounds, even thousands on – smoke. There is a regular case-history pattern in one of the toughest professions, where smoking is extremely popular – the Army – that shows apparently highly fit and strong men having major heart attacks and many die in their thirties. Almost without noticing, they have smoked 150,000 cigarettes in 20 years.

How would you answer a parent who put all these (and other) arguments to you? Should you bother if your clothes and rooms that other members of the family use smell smoky? Is it possible to reach a compromise?

But, of course, the issue may be quite the reverse. You may be wanting your **parents** to stop smoking.

h) **Noise**: If playing records or guitars or computer games annoy your parents, how far should you ration the time or the volume? Are there noisy activities in which they take part? Can you explain why most parties have music that's so loud any sustained conversation is impossible? How would you persuade your parents to hold a party, at your house, with a disco?

i) **Television**: Do you think families are thrown together too much with the television dominating the sitting room? Does television or video bring you closer to your parents as something you both share? If there are arguments about how much television you should watch or which programmes should be on, how do you go about solving them?

j) **Homework**: Do your parents nag you about homework? Why? If they leave you to get on with your own work, do you have a good space and a quiet length of time to do it? If not, what could you do to give yourself more time, peace and space? (e.g. working at school? at the local library? at a friend's house? early morning? at a regular, agreed quiet time?)

k) **Quarrelling**: What do you find particularly irritating about your brothers and/or sisters? What do you think they find particularly irritating about you? If you were your parents, would you referee the quarrels differently? Do you think your parents have favourites or are inconsistent? Why? If you can give your parents an example of inconsistent treatment, would they be prepared to discuss it?

l) **Table manners**: How much would you ask your children or children you were looking after to eat quietly; eat what is served to them; keep their elbows off the table; sit while they were eating; wait at the table till everyone had finished? What would you do if they, belched; picked their teeth; read a book; combed their hair; played with their food; grabbed other people's food? Make a list of the things that you would find most offensive: does it fit with the habits that your parents object to? Food and meals can quickly become a battleground where people get back at each other for real or imaginary insults – it may be hard to say openly that your mother irritates you or makes too many demands on you: it's very easy to imply this by refusing to eat what she's cooked. You may not like the way your father bosses you around (as you see it), so an easy way of undermining him is to behave insolently (as he sees it) at a meal, especially if there are visitors. How can you get beyond these 'games' and discuss the real issues that are causing conflict?

m) **Money**: Make a list in three columns: what you are given and what you earn in column 1 (every week); what you spend in column 2 (with rough categories – clothes, records, food, fares, etc.); what you would like to spend in column 3 with rough but realistic categories. Compare the lists each of you has compiled. How far does column 3 differ from column 2? Is it a source of deep resentment or something you are prepared to accept? If column 2 and column 1 are quite different for various members of the group, this could be another source of resentment – perhaps another focus for arguments, so it is important that the leader of the group is sensitive to any feelings of bitterness when a 'rich' member of the group seems to have done nothing to deserve such good fortune, and may even boast about it. Finally, what attitude do you take and what do you say to someone who says, 'I'm not bothering with all this: when I want something, I steal it'?

n) **Staying in bed late**: Would you be happier if you were allowed total freedom to get up when you liked, not only at weekends, but for schooldays? How much should parents dictate to you what your timetable is at home? Do there seem to be different standards for different people in the house? Why?

o) & p) **Hogging the phone/bathroom**: Is the problem caused by money, again – i.e. you don't contribute to the phone bill? If so, how much should you pay? Should you have to ask before you use it? Should you make an effort to keep calls short and only phone in cheap periods? How can you arrange for the people who most like or need some part of the house to have a fair share?

Now let your leader report back to the whole class. If there's time the discussion can open out between the 'reporters'.

■ *EXERCISE*

20 minutes × 2 – individually, when working in pairs

a) Select from the list below the words which you think apply to you and number them 1 (if sometimes true), 2 (if often true), 3 (if always true). (Check with your teacher or look up in a dictionary the words you're not familiar with.)

amiable	affectionate	agreeable	animated	argumentative
aggressive	apathetic	antagonistic	benign	belligerent
calm	conceited	critical	carping	defensive
dull	dreary	dutiful	efficient	enthusiastic
extravagant	foolish	friendly	flattering	fastidious
grumbling	garrulous	happy	harsh	healthy
hateful	inconsistent	inconsiderate	irritating	jolly
jaded	kind	loyal	lazy	lenient
morbid	morose	neat	noisy	nagging
obedient	obstinate	petty	prejudiced	pleasant
provocative	quiet	quick-tempered	reasonable	rotten
sly	stubborn	strict	timid	satisfied
trusting	temperate	unhelpful	understanding	vain
vulgar	wasteful	wicked	young	zealous

b) How far would your parents agree with this list? Say where they'd disagree and why?

c) Show the list to your partner (preferably somebody who knows you well) and see if he or she agrees with your own estimates. Discuss where there are big discrepancies between the score you've given yourself and what your partner would give you.

d) Now change over. Discuss your partner's scores and say how far you agree with them and why.

e) Select the words in this list which particularly apply to your parents. Number their main qualities, as you see them – 1, 2 and 3 – as you did for yourself.

f) Discuss with your partner whether your parents would accept this assessment. If not, why would they assess themselves differently?

(The ideal follow-up to this exercise is to discuss your self-evaluation with your parents and your evaluation of them with them, too. Unfortunately, a lot of parents may feel this is (a) nothing to do with you, and/or (b) nothing to do with the school, so you will have to be diplomatic. Nobody is going to want to be assessed as rotten, nagging and wicked at strength 3! So, think about why you may feel so strongly and what you can do to suggest that you may have faults, before launching into other people's.)

Role play

Take any of the topics that interest you and, in pairs, act out a discussion between parent and son/daughter where there is a basic disagreement about this topic: to make sure it's not just a shouting match, try to follow this rough outline:

a) Start in a neutral situation (e.g. exchanging the odd word while watching television, making breakfast, washing-up).

b) Start discussing a minor problem (e.g. how good one of the actors is on television, whether breakfast cereals are too expensive, why it would be worth having an automatic washing-up machine).

c) Lead on to the issue that's really causing friction.

d) Bring in other areas of disagreement.

e) Have a 'safety-valve' – e.g. one of you must be able to walk out, save face or feel some sort of justification by making points that aren't just angry but also strongly put and fair.

Then reverse the situation, so that the son/daughter becomes the parent, the parent becomes the son/daughter: it would also help if the grievance changes from one person to the other, so that it's possible to see that an adult can be just as hurt and frustrated as an adolescent.

Good improvisations can be shown to the rest of the class; even if you're not getting very far, show a minute of the action, so that other people can appreciate what you've done.

Discuss where you felt sympathy with each of the people arguing: if you felt no sympathy at all for one side, it was a bad improvisation or a caricature of 'the enemy'. Suggest how the dispute you saw could be resolved.

Solutions?

We've deliberately not played the role of 'agony aunts' because every conflict in the home feels unique and different from any we could suggest here. Sometimes there is no solution until one of the people moves away or changes completely, but before that happens, it must help to see your 'enemy' not as a mad, bad and stupid monster but as someone who's probably been conditioned, like you, to think in certain ways by upbringing, circumstances, bad luck or good luck – it's very unlikely that one side of an argument is prejudiced and irrational, while the other is objective and completely logical. Families are the most powerful unit positively and negatively, for building people up and tearing them down, so you need all your ability to communicate and, at times, act, to turn a confrontation into a compromise. If you can, at least, put into words some of the frustration that these issues cause, you can begin to have a common ground of arguing and protesting – otherwise, you're just shouting and fighting in the dark.

Meeting half-way

We hope you can quote conversations within your families where opposing points of view have been presented, a compromise has been reached and an argument resolved!

2 School protest

'He's always picking on me.' 'She's got no right to tell me to do that.' 'Of course, what can you expect? Teachers only like creeps.' 'If she says that to me again, I'm going to walk out.' 'You can't trust him.'

Disagreements with teachers, like disagreements with parents, are usually not about the immediate problem – missed homework, rudeness, boring lessons, apparently pointless regulations. Underneath, there's likely to be a basic difference of opinion about how students and teachers see themselves. A student tends to want more self-expression, more freedom, more chance to impress or talk with people he/she likes and admires; a teacher has the difficult task of trying to give 20 or 30 people a chance for self-expression. Freedom has to fit the existing institution, and some teachers may feel that any loss of control, particularly in drama or discussions, means anarchy, so they don't allow the situation to arise. This can mean that talk and self-assertion are thought of as a 'social' activity, which may not be encouraged in the classroom.

Stage 1: So, you have to decide how to resolve a disagreement and what moves you are going to make. If you object to what a teacher says to you or about you, the first person to approach is the teacher – not by trying to sabotage the lesson, but by discussing the problem, in private, afterwards. Most teachers are impressed by someone who takes the trouble to ask questions about the way the subject is taught or the class is run. As long as they are asked politely why things have to be done this way, teachers are prepared to explain. In other words, generalise the question – don't start off by 'it's not fair . . .', ask for the teacher's opinion: 'I'm sorry I find this subject difficult, but could you go a bit slower?' 'Do you think we could have more discussion?' 'How much time should homework take?'. Suppose the issue is homework: if it takes you three hours to do a piece of work, you need to know:

a) Is this what the teacher would expect?

b) If it is, how often would it be reasonable to set so much, when there are six or seven other subjects to do? (A timetable drawn up to show your work times would be impressive evidence.)

c) If it isn't, what's taking too long? Perhaps you're copying out useless material, spending too long worrying, taking hours to make a drawing look neat – go over the work and how you do it, with the teacher.

At the end of a discussion like this, you should feel that you know how to work more productively and the teacher should feel that you've taken a very positive interest in your work. You've collaborated in private so you should have more respect for each other in public, if there's another problem arising.

Be polite: thank a teacher who has taken extra time to help you, whatever your prejudices. If a teacher gave everyone that amount of time, he or she would be working seven or eight times as long, every week, so don't underestimate the pressures on them. Try to keep the discussion impersonal – talk about the work, reather than the unrest or other personalities.

Stage 2: You may find it embarrassing to approach the teacher who seems to have humiliated you. If you've been rude or aggressive it is not easy to begin a new discussion. To avoid a feud, you need an arbitrator – most schools have some formal or informal mechanism to settle this sort of conflict. Find out what happens in yours – who are the umpires? They may be a form teacher, a counsellor, a head of year, a head of school, a deputy head or a sympathetic teacher who is easy to talk to, and who might be prepared to intervene in a dispute. If all these words like 'dispute', 'arbitrator', 'mechanism' sound like parts of a news item on a strike, it's simply because there are no magic methods which work in school that aren't relevant outside it. All the arguments that blow up in an industrial strike are eventually settled by the same processes as you can use in a school, though obviously it's better to settle them informally and courteously, instead of starting a campaign. The body which usually comes into big disputes where the parties are completely entrenched is called ACAS, short for Arbitration, Conciliation and Advisory Service. The words of its title sum up the process you need to follow:
– find someone who can judge ('arbitrate') between the two points of view;

– find someone who can reconcile you ('conciliate');
and hope that the same person can advise both of you on how to avoid another major disagreement.

Stage 3: Though we hope you won't reach this stage in any protest, you may feel that the people in school are unlikely to appreciate your point of view; as the arbitrators in Stage 2 are teachers you may not feel assured of them looking objectively at what's happened. Even if you like them as individuals, you make feel that they are always going to serve the institution rather than you. At this point, you ought to stop and think: is this protest more important than the institution? Is the school (or Further Education College or whatever form of institution) going to be failing everyone, not just you, if this injustice is allowed? If you feel that you must continue protesting, as a matter of principle, then you must work out a strategy.

What's wrong with this? Will they ever understand one another's point of view?

By consulting many of the people below, or by researching the structure of your institution, you ought to build up a picture of how decisions are made. Here is one possible model of a chain of command:

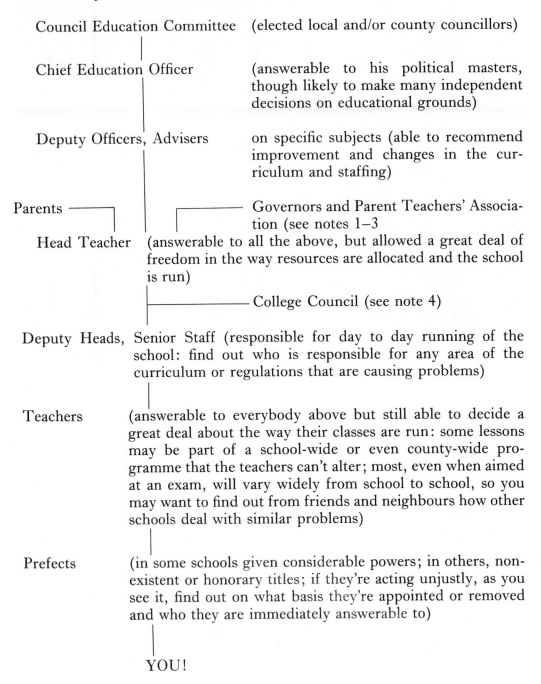

Council Education Committee   (elected local and/or county councillors)

Chief Education Officer   (answerable to his political masters, though likely to make many independent decisions on educational grounds)

Deputy Officers, Advisers   on specific subjects (able to recommend improvement and changes in the curriculum and staffing)

Parents ———

——— Governors and Parent Teachers' Association (see notes 1–3

Head Teacher   (answerable to all the above, but allowed a great deal of freedom in the way resources are allocated and the school is run)

——— College Council (see note 4)

Deputy Heads, Senior Staff (responsible for day to day running of the school: find out who is responsible for any area of the curriculum or regulations that are causing problems)

Teachers   (answerable to everybody above but still able to decide a great deal about the way their classes are run: some lessons may be part of a school-wide or even county-wide programme that the teachers can't alter; most, even when aimed at an exam, will vary widely from school to school, so you may want to find out from friends and neighbours how other schools deal with similar problems)

Prefects   (in some schools given considerable powers; in others, non-existent or honorary titles; if they're acting unjustly, as you see it, find out on what basis they're appointed or removed and who they are immediately answerable to)

YOU!

How does this chain of command correspond with your school?

How will this be argued out?

1) Parents, in most cases, are your best allies, and good head teachers will take time to listen to them. But try to have a constructive talk first with a senior teacher whom you feel you can approach and thus possibly avoid involving the Head Teacher.

2) The amount of power exercised by Parent Teachers' Associations varies considerably – some schools don't have one at all (through indifference or deliberate policy) and some schools take a great deal of notice of them. In fact a good PTA is a reliable measurement of a school's successful co-operation with parents.

3) The influence of Governors can be vital. The governing body usually contains a parent governor, a teacher governor and a student governor – so you might consult any of these people to help you. The Governing body appoints teachers, makes recommendations to the local authority and influences the way a school is run.

4) Finally there may be a school or college council made up of student representatives, who can meet and make representations to the Head Teacher. If there is not then you must find another channel. Prefects? Public debate? Assembly?

In any sensitive institution there should be opportunities for mutual discussion to 'clear the air' or resolve grievances.

So if you want to make an effective protest, work through the power structure, keeping careful records of what you have asked, and what you have been told.

Solutions?

If all discussion fails the last resort might be to change schools or leave school completely. If this is to be considered try to take a long view. We are facing you with this very extreme case, because in any argument of principle, it's important to decide how far you will take it. Is it so important that you must move through all the stages outlined above? In most cases, it shouldn't have become so important – reconciliation early on would be a much more productive use of time. But, if you have a cause that must be pursued, find out the stages in your particular school that will bring it to the attention of the appropriate people – and *listen* to what they say. They have dealt with hundreds of students and, in the long term, however inconvenient their ruling is now, they may be acting in everyone's best interest, including yours. But you should feel, by the end of the protest, that you know why decisions are made and where you and the Establishment stand even it it's as far apart as ever. It probably won't be, because you've once again established common ground for talking, instead of walls and fortifications for sniping at each other.

3 Neighbourhood protest

Take one of the situations below and in *one minute* make a complaint to the rest of the group, who will listen to all your points then answer them, explaining, refusing or pointing out the prejudice in your argument:

1) Criticise your neighbours who have neglected their dog.
   YOU: the dog-lover.
   THE GROUP: The neighbouring family.

2) Challenge a shop-keeper who has overcharged you.
   YOU: the customer.
   THE GROUP: Shop-keeper, cashier or other customers.

3) Complain to the Council about a local danger-spot – e.g. a disused canal

which ought to be filled in because several children have been injured playing near it.

YOU: The parent of an injured child.

THE GROUP: Council members.

4) Protest about shops being closed on Sundays.

YOU: A customer or shop-keeper.

THE GROUP: Councillors or members of the Lord's Day Observance Society or other groups who believe Sunday should be for religion and recreation, not making money.

Arguing it out: who will they follow?

5) Demand that the Council provide better play equipment in the local playground.

YOU: The parent or equipment user.

THE GROUP: Council members who have already had bills of several hundred pounds for vandalised equipment.

6) Protest to the local housing committee because there are no homes for young newly married couples.

YOU: Someone about to get married, wanting to leave home.

THE GROUP: Members of the housing committee who are anxious knowing that increased rates will lose them their place on the Council.

7) Demand that your local MP do something about unemployment among school-leavers.
   YOU: The school-leaver.
   THE GROUP: The MP and several of his constituents, who are faced with rising rates bills, taxes and smaller profit-margins in their businesses.

8) Condemn the plans to turn a local quarry into a disposal ground for nuclear waste.
   YOU: Local resident.
   THE GROUP: Electricity Board engineers who see the only way of providing enough energy for the National Grid as nuclear power.

9) Object to a new motorway or bypass which will cut across your neighbourhood.
   YOU: Local resident.
   THE GROUP: Motorists and lorry drivers who are constantly delayed by the narrow road that they have to use at present.

10) Ask a shop-keeper to stop selling fireworks because you know that several children have been injured recently by playing with fireworks.
    YOU: The parent.
    THE GROUP: The shop-keeper and people who want to go on buying fireworks for properly supervised private parties and displays.

These are just a few suggestions; haranguing people may work it out of your system, but it doesn't get you very far. The group will quickly close ranks against you, refuse to admit that any of your arguments are valid and the whole exercise will end in shouting or silence.

For instance, if you tried the first situation, you might have said something like – 'I've been listening to that dog whining and howling for three nights. What's the matter with you? Can't you hear it? Why do you leave it out all night? It's freezing. How would you like to shiver in a freezing shed? You've never tried it – why don't you get someone to lock you out. Maybe you'd start to think about that poor bloody animal . . .'

A more positive approach to the next-door neighbours would be a factual one – even though it's hard to be unemotional. Ask them if they know their dog is making a noise: it's just possible they don't. Ask them if they know it's distressed and distressing to you: it doesn't occur to some people that their neighbours might react differently to things they take for granted.

Ask them if there's any way you can help – e.g. taking the dog out for exercise. If you've suggested a number of positive points, it's harder for the owner to see you as a threat, who must be got rid of as soon as possible.

Stage 2: Maybe the polite approach produces no reaction. Then, as with disputes in the school section, you will need some local help. Ask other neighbours if they're disturbed by the noise. If they are, ask them if they could contact the owner, too. Several people making the same firm but polite objections to what's happening can be very impressive – most people don't want to alienate the whole road, though they may not care about offending one or two neighbours. A petition signed by at least three people who are concerned is not only evidence for a public nuisance, it will be enough for the police or other official bodies to take action – you are clearly not just a pernickety complainer, if other people support you. Photocopy the petition and then show it to the person who is causing the nuisance.

Stage 3: If all this unofficial action produces no result, you are probably going to need to bring in official help. In the case of the neglected dog, you'd do best to call at, or telephone, the RSPCA (address and phone number in your local phone book or from the local library). Report the details carefully and courteously: for example,

'I'm Margaret Robinson of 15 Beech Road. I want to report the people at number 23. They have a dog which they lock out at night without any proper shelter. The dog's howling most of the night and it disturbs the neighbours. During the day, the dog's allowed to roam the street and scrounges for food, overturning the dustbins and ripping up the dustbin bags . . .'

The RSPCA may want to take more information and should then report back to you, once they've taken action. All this will take time and patience, but, in the end, the dog is likely to be much better than if you'd simply gone rushing round with a string of abusive remarks.

Look at number 2

The negative approach: 'Hang on. Didn't I just give you a £5 note? This change is wrong. You've got a nerve. Don't try that on me. I'm not that stupid . . .' You get angry, rightly, but you don't give the shop-keeper any time to defend himself. Maybe it was a mistake. Maybe it was a deliberate piece of cheating. Obviously, the shop-keeper isn't going to admit the second possibility, but if you want to use the shop again and get any sort of service, you can go about your protest more tactfully.

The positive approach: 'Can I just check the change?' (Show what you've been given and count it together.) 'I think that's a mistake. I didn't give you £5 I gave you a £10 note. Look, it's there (pointing to till compartment; wait for shop-keeper to put this right; if they still don't) 'I definitely gave you £10; if you don't believe me, ask this lady' (or any other witness; if there isn't a witness, ask for the person's name and say that you'll lodge a complaint, either with their boss or the local Chamber of Commerce or the police; it's unlikely that they'll want to argue further).

Look at number 3

Try this exercise using powers of persuasion and explanation. You need to get to know the facts and these might lead you to think out ways in which the reform could take place. The facts might also lead you to co-operate with the powers-that-be instead of opposing them.

Any solving of this problem would demand negotiation with important authorities and investigation of the following facts:

1) Is the stretch of canal part of a longer 'working' canal?
2) What would happen to the 'feed in' water if it were blocked?
3) To whom does the canal belong?
4) Who is responsible for the banks and tow paths?
5) Is there any protective railing?
6) Are parents responsible for checking and protecting their children?

Might not the whole situation be reversed and the neglected dangerous canal be made into a place of beauty and pleasure? Suggest what could be done. Could adolescents 'adopt' it; keeping it clean and tidy; manning playgrounds; helping with children's games; planting trees and flowers.

Any protest to the Council is best submitted formally as a petition with as many signatures as you can get supporting your complaint or appeal.

Prevent the problem before it gets out of hand; here are some issues which involve protest, but which will be a lot easier to solve the more constructive ideas you include at an early stage.

Discussion

Divide into your groups of four or five choosing a leader who will later be your spokesman.

Discuss any reforms, improvements, services or gadgets which would add to the well-being, safety or health of any section of the community.

To start you talking, here are a few aspects of living where much help is needed. (You may have other ideas or you may want to take just one point in the following to amplify it.)

Group 1: Vandalism and violence

1) Can you think of any ways in which vandalism could be checked?
2) Can you offer practical suggestions for catching the culprits?
3) Make suggestions for what you think might be appropriate punishment. For example, should those who destroy be made to repair and restore property?
4) How can the police be helped in their difficult task?
5) Can you devise any gadget or system for protecting, for example, telephone kiosks?

6) Why do people become violent? Suggest different ways of using their energy and working off temper.

Group 2: *Long term prevention of vandalism and violence*

1) If there were better facilities for young people's activities do you think this would reduce vandalism? Suggest the kind of facilities the town or borough should provide.
2) Do you think that schools and colleges should be open community centres so that their facilities could be used in the evenings and weekends? If so, how would you man them?
3) Should all young people do a year's community service after they leave school with a large range of options – e.g. hospital work; farming; helping with the handicapped; looking after our parks and public places; helping in nursery schools and old people's homes, etc.?
4) Should people have to 'earn' their unemployment money?

Group 3: *Old people*

1) Blind people have white sticks – a simple device for making the public aware of their plight. Can you think of any other gadgets to help those who cannot get themselves about?
2) 'Meals on Wheels' was a spendid idea devised and carried out by the Women's Voluntary Service. Can you suggest other practical forms of help for the house-bound or bed-ridden?
3) Old people are in great danger with gas and electrical appliances as well as with open fires. Can you think of any safety devices?
4) Transport is expensive; shopping difficult. Can you think of any services which could be provided by shop-keepers and young people?
5) There are a great many benefits which old people can get through the State if they *know* about them. (Unfortunately those who know all the perks are very often those who don't need them.) Can you think of ways in which the young could help older people to get the appropriate passes and vouchers and help them to fill up the necessary forms?
6) Are there any ways in which elderly retired people with various skills could help young people?

Group 4: *Damaged lives*

This covers a wide range of needy people so you may only be able to consider one or two groups in this session. Here are a few headings:

a) Blind
b) Deaf
c) Crippled
d) Spastic
e) War casualties
f) Victims of terrorists

g) Orphans, homeless or neglected children

h) Drug addicts

i) Incurables (terminal patients)

j) Mentally or physically disabled

Think out some apparatus or service which would help any of these unfortunate people.

Discuss: a) how the government could give further help;
b) how young people could help;
c) how 'early retired' people could help.

Group 5: *Giving the town or village a 'face lift'*

1) Are there any eye-sores in your town?
   How would you suggest that the town is made more beautiful? tidier? cleaner?
   Could young people play any part in this; if so, in what way?
2) Are there any interesting old buildings or things of historical interest which are being pulled down?
   Could you find out why they are being demolished and whether they could be preserved?
3) Are the new buildings worthy of the town?
   Are they part of an imaginative plan?
   or: Have they just been put up at random by speculative builders?
   Discuss between you (and write it down) a petition for either:
   a) a new arts centre, or
   b) a bypass road to keep through traffic out of the town centre, or
   c) a change of traffic control at a danger point, or
   d) a traffic-free shopping precinct, or
   e) a sports or youth centre.

Each group chooses *one* idea from their discussion and their spokesman presents it to the whole class.

Each bill or petition will open up for debate and questions from the class. It will then be voted for adoption and passed if it is proved to be a practical proposition. Remember that it is no use simply 'kite-flying', the proposition must be logistically and economically viable.

N.B. The projects discussed in this session would require considerable following up. You would need to consult various authorities through and with your members of staff. If this is achieved then you could invite a local councillor – or someone associated with welfare projects – or your local MP, to listen to your proposition and to answer questions.

Organisations which will help you in practical application of your ideas:
Women's Voluntary Service
Townswomen's Guild (Social Service Section)
Soroptimist Club
National Business & Professional Women's Clubs
Rotary Club
Round Table Club
League of Pity
Save the Children
NSPCC
Old People's Welfare
Town and Country Planning
Samaritans
Women's Institute

You can obtain the local addresses from your reference library or publicity and information centre.

If you're not sure which organisation would be the most appropriate, start with the Citizens' Advice Bureau, who can offer specialist advice and put you in touch with the right person very quickly, if you need the backing of a particular organisation. Many organisations are glad to answer questions and may even send a speaker to your school, if it's an issue which concerns a lot of the students. In the end, you may need to enlist the help of your local MP. Most give 'surgeries' to their constituents – and you're a constituent, who will very soon have a vote. Many MPs recognise that today's protesters and debaters are tomorrow's voters and opinion-formers and some actively encourage more informed debate among young people – for instance, they will arrange trips around the House of Commons, answer questions on local issues in public or private correspondence and take the trouble to visit youth centres, schools and local community groups. Greville Janner, MP for a Leicester constituency, invited all the young people in the city's secondary schools in his division to put forward ideas which would help to make the country a better place. He received 400 suggestions, from which he chose the idea that old and disabled people on their own should be able to flash a distress signal to get immediate help. This proposal was then put forward as a 'Private Member's Bill' in Parliament.

To conclude this protest chapter, it is worth explaining how a suggestion from someone in a school like yours can go through the various stages which might ultimately affect the way everyone lives. Once an MP has taken up an issue and decided it's sufficiently important to present to Parliament as a private bill, he has to do a great deal of negotiating and lobbying, and he will welcome publicity from his supporters which presents his case to the general public in a positive and informed way. There is great competition to get a bill 'heard' (i.e. debated in Parliament) and the MP has to take his turn on the waiting list. Eventually, the examiner of private bills may accept the bill and give it a certificate. The bill is then deposited in the Private Bill Office and presented for the first 'reading'. Then follows a second reading, after which the bill is sent to a select committee where every clause and every word is scrutinised. Then it is returned to the House of Commons for a third reading. After this, the same procedure is repeated in the House of Lords. In each case, debate follows which may produce amendments. Then there is a final vote, and what may have started as *one person's* protest becomes part of our permanent constitutional law.

Solutions in a democratic country

Only a few Private Members' Bills ever become law, and each one proposed has thousands of supporters, so how democratic is such a competitive and pressurised system? Although pressure groups increasingly influence opinion and operate very sophisticated publicity campaigns, they are composed of protesters, all of whom once felt isolated and ignored. By open discussion and considerate argument, they have shown that there is still a point in practising and defending free speech. Hence the title of this book: *Direct Speech*.

10 Speaking in a formal setting

Running a committee meeting

If you have attended committee meetings you may agree with the cynic who said: 'The best number for a committee is two – with one absent.' There is so often so much pointless waffle at meetings and the glib and garrulous often score if the Chairman is not astute in bringing each person into the discussion. Perhaps people go to meetings simply because they like being with other people. Others like to feel important.

The only genuine reason for having a committee is to reach decisions and act on them.

If you are on a committee in school, college or an outside organisation, ask yourself what the *purpose* of your meeting is. It may be one, or all three of these, for example:

1) To define what you are aiming at and to make decisions.
2) To share information.
3) To make each 'committed' member contribute towards a particular goal.

1 Procedure

a) The chairman and secretary should go carefully through a prepared agenda. The secretary will be convening the meeting and sending out the agenda.
b) There should be a reason for each item, noting whether the particular item is for information, discussion or resolution.
c) How many people should be at the meeting? The smaller the group the more intense can be the discussion. On the other hand if it is too small it may not be representative.
d) If decisions need background information this should be made available beforehand so that people can do their homework. People cannot be expected to read pages of information at the committee table so send brief memos prior to the meeting.
e) The chairman should decide on the order of items very carefully. Substantial items should be discussed when everyone is fresh, immediately after the formal signing of the previous meeting's minutes and 'business

arising'. Some kind of time limit can be put on individual items, otherwise later items on the agenda can be given short shrift.

f) Experts agree that 1½ hours is long enough for any meeting. One hour should be the limit for any school committee meeting.

2 *You as a Chairman*

In addition to the previous points, look at these:

a) Don't talk too much. You are there to *listen* and direct.

b) Think of yourself as a servant of the group, but be firm with people who want to hog the discussion.

c) See the issues clearly – it is too easy for a meeting to get side-tracked. Smell out the 'red herrings' and 'net' them!

d) Sum up clearly and concisely after each item on the agenda so that members know exactly what point has been reached and what decisions and results have been reached. If a resolution is to be minuted it should be proposed, seconded and agreed. This summing up will help the secretary to make accurate minutes.

e) Do not offend; you can be kind as well as firm. You have an important social role to play, so make sure that the shy people have a chance to speak and that weak people are not demolished. *Ask* quiet people for their opinions.

3 *You as a Secretary*

a) Your job is to see that all arrangements for venue, date and decisions are put on paper and distributed.

b) You convene the meeting and send out the agenda which gives the precise time and place of the meeting.

c) You take the 'minutes'. Strictly speaking a 'minute' is a recorded fact of a motion which should be followed by a 'resolution'. This should be proposed, seconded and 'carried' (by a show of hands). Do not try to record everything that is said. Reduce the discussion and chatter to simple facts: e.g. 'After a lengthy discussion it was decided that the Anfield Rock Band event for the charity "Live Aid" should be held in the School Hall on Saturday 8 March 1987.' (Proposed by Arthur Benson and Seconded by Christine Davenport.)

d) You type out the minutes as soon as possible after the meeting, and copies are distributed to the members, or (according to your society rules) one copy is read out by you at the following meeting.

The above guidelines are only an outline sketch for committee procedure. For more detailed information on resolutions, amendments, etc., consult your library. A completely comprehensive 'classic' book which also covers company meetings and Parliamentary debates written by a former legal advisor to the

Trades Union Congress is: *ABC of Chairmanship* by Lord Citrine published by NCLC Publishing Society Ltd, 11 Dartmouth Street, London SW1H 9BN. Don't be misled by the 'ABC', the book goes through every professional intricate detail and is in no sense 'simple'.

Your part in formal argument: debating

So far in this book your discussions have been in small informal groups where speakers have been able to pick up a cue and speak in any order. Even in a formal committee this is still in order. In controlled debate however, there are prescribed techniques and formalities which make the occasion more of an intellectual exercise than a spontaneous expression of opinion. Your school may run a debating society or conduct mock elections; if you are to take part effectively you will need to know the order of procedure and the thinking processes which are necessary for logical presentation of your facts.

Debating subjects

All debates have a theme presented in the form of a positive statement (called the 'motion') which begins with: 'That' for example:

Motion:
- 'That wearing school uniform restricts individuality and should be abolished'
- 'That a year of community service should be obligatory between the ages of 16 and 20'
- 'That the rating system should be more fairly spread to include all wage-earners'
- 'That bicycles should be taxed and registered'
- 'That grant-aid should be equal for all 16+ students'
- 'That identity cards should be compulsory for football supporters'

These are all serious subjects but many societies include in their programme a light-hearted one which sharpens wit and witticism, e.g.

- 'That churches should be closed on Sunday'
- 'That there should be a "*young* age pension"'

Having decided on the motion, two or three main speakers should be chosen to represent each side of the argument: the 'pros' and 'cons'. Each one should then do his homework and research to prepare opening statements in collaboration with the other members of the chosen team. Although a debate is more worthwhile if the speakers really believe in what they are saying and speak with conviction, it is a useful intellectual exercise to line up arguments against your own beliefs and sometimes have to speak on the other side, acting as 'devil's advocate'.

1 Order of procedure

a) For every debate there is a Chairman who calls on the 'original' speaker to present the motion and argue in its favour for an agreed length of time. Most societies arrange a definite time (e.g. five minutes, but ten minutes would be a maximum allotment).

b) The original speaker may call on a member of his team (or in the second or third round a speaker from the floor) to support the motion.

c) The opposition follows the same procedure.

d) After equal opportunities for both sides have been given by the Chairman, he then calls on –

e) The original speaker to have the final say and to reiterate his support of the motion.

f) The Chairman then sums up and the motion is put to the vote with 'Ayes' and 'Nos' or with a show of hands:

   'All those in favour of the motion please say "Aye" (or show hands)'

   'All those against the motion, please say "No" (or a show of hands)'

   Note that it is human nature to enjoy shouting but the word 'No' has more carrying power then 'Aye' so it might be as well to check with a show of hands.

2 Preparation before the debate

a) Collect your material under two headings: facts and opinions. In both cases be able to support your facts and opinions with your source. If it is purely your *own* opinion, say so:

   'In my opinion ...' but if you have also an authoritative source too, then add it to your own.

   'In my opinion (which I may say is also that of Lord Denning) ...'

b) Check that your facts are:
   1) clear (short and taut; use graphic words);
   2) reliable (check your sources);
   3) relevant (keep to the point);
   4) valid (give a source or support which makes it an unarguable truth).

c) Check that your opinions are:
   1) first hand. If they are second-hand give your source.
   2) Explain the authority on which the opinion is based.
   3) Give clear reasons for holding this opinion yourself (quote your own experience).

3 Presenting your argument

REASONING: your argument must be reasonable, topical and persuasive. Generally speaking there are two ways of reasoning: either by *deduction* or *induction*.

a) **Deduction** is reasoning from the general to the particular. Look out because you can lose the point with blanket generalisations – e.g. 'Socrates said: "All Greeks are liars" (but Socrates was a Greek, therefore what he said was not true, therefore all Greeks are not liars . . .)'.

But it might be possible to say: 'All cyclists are road users, it is estimated that there are . . . of them. If each one should contribute £5 to the cost of road maintenance this would bring in . . .'

b) **Induction** is reasoning from the particular case to the general: 'I know an old lady in my street living alone on a pension who was attacked by a violent youth. She had no means of calling for help and subsequently died. There are hundreds of old ladies in this plight. I appeal to you to support this motion which will ensure that simple alarms are installed in every home where the elderly are living on their own.'

c) **Rhetorical questions** – powerful reasoning and persuasion can stem from the rhetorical question which is thrown out to the listeners but which is not answered:

   – 'Who are these "top people" who qualify for these huge salaries?'
   – 'Do people of such high esteem and competence need to be bribed?'
   – 'What does the marriage status ensure? Marital bliss? Protection of children? Financial equality?'

The rhetorical question is useful because you can cause your opponent's points to be put in doubt: if, for example, you were *against* the road tax for cyclists you could challenge with a rhetorical question: 'Has the speaker for this motion worked out the methods and cost of collecting this tax? Would it not cost more to get in than it would produce?'

Here is a good use of a rhetorical question on nationalisation: 'It implies that we propose to nationalise everything, but do we? Everything? – the whole of light industry, the whole of agriculture, all the shops, every little pub and garage? Of course not. We have long ago come to accept a mixed economy; in which case, if this is our view – as I believe it to be of 90% of the Labour Party – had we not better say so instead of going out of our way to court misrepresentation?' (Aneurin Bevan speaking at a Labour Party Conference.)

d) **Reasoning by analogy** – In this case you take a comparison and bring it down in your favour. If, for example, you were **for** the motion on the road tax for cyclists, you could cite a country where this is in operation and quote the income produced from the tax.

Be on the look-out for weak argument on the opposing side: If statistics are quoted, are they from a reliable source and if so are they *relevant* to the present argument?

Notice if the argument is just appealing to the emotions or is an exaggerated sweeping statement: e.g. in the cycle tax motion – 'Well it's a rotten country that takes money from kids', *or* 'That will mean our newspapers won't be delivered'.

GENERAL ATTITUDE AND MANNER IN DEBATE: Keep alert. Have paper and pencil for reminder notes; keep calm; be good-tempered and occasionally humorous; be sincere but not too intense. Give yourself *pauses* in which to reflect, to be received, to emphasise and relax. Make eye-ball to eye-ball contact with your listeners. Don't *read-talk*. Make a few firm convincing points rather than a number of weak ones and try to have a forceful word at the end of each statement:

e.g. *Not*: Children would benefit from nursery school physically and mentally if this bill is introduced

But: I appeal to you to support this bill to ensure that this nation leads the world in nurturing its children.

(Notice the rhythmic power of the key words; the most important word is the final one.)

Formal discussions on newspaper topics

Do we read newspapers or just headlines

Nowadays people often hear news bulletins several times a day on radio and television and by the time they buy a paper the news is not 'new'. So people buy newspapers for different reasons: political opinion; personality gossip; regular features by popular writers; fashion and 'pop'; crosswords; glamorous photographs; advertisements (especially local papers); radio and TV programmes ...

Very often the casual buyer is attracted by the street news posters:
– 'Local MP scandal'

– 'Charles criticises architects'
– 'Bomb scare in Oxford Street'
– 'Film-star murder suspect'
or catches sight of the front page headline:
– 'Princess: Stormy reception' (anticlimax when the reader finds this reference was to the weather!)

Space restriction demands that headlines should be brief and compact and composed at speed. It is not surprising, therefore, that many are misleading and ambiguous:

– 'Soccer fan gets life for riot and assault' ('life' is life imprisonment and he was not *only* a soccer fan!)
– 'Mobs riot after hanging' (suggests either resurrection or mortality!)
– 'Axe to fall on timber workers' (metaphor or reality?)
– 'Worms in peanut butter jar customers' (is jar a noun or a verb?)
– 'McArthur flies back to front' (A famous one in the Second World War)

Headlines within the paper

Headlines aim to be short and eye-catching. The fewer the number of letters the larger and bolder the type can be.

As an exercise in clarity and projection go quickly round the class saying *one* headline so that it will be heard, received and remembered.

Here are ten headlines from the *Daily Telegraph* of 26 October 1985; they show the ingenuity, and often cunning, of the 'caption' writer.

a) Marsh launches British attack on Europeans
b) Soviets admit errors
c) Ailing police chief to go
d) First jets land at Knock
e) Mr Reagan's agenda
f) Kasparov has title in grasp
g) Coach baiting
h) Royals hit back
i) Misconceptions on common land
j) Broadmoor for 'vampire' killer

How many of these strike you as interesting and worth following up – why?
Headlines (a, f and h) – which all have aggressive words in them: 'attack', 'grasp', 'hit back' – are, in fact, all about sport: boxing, chess and baseball.

Now look at these ten headlines from the *Sun* of 30 November 1985.

a) Elton in £2 million hit records victory
b) Hatton fired from panto

c) Berlei Bras go bust
d) TV girl's romance at a demo
e) Jesus banned for Christmas
f) Kiss girl a Rambo hotshot
g) Family is wiped out by blast
h) Cilla's no sex dates
i) I knifed police spy in terror
j) Taylor in bust-up

Is it fair to say that the only appeals consistently used in these headlines play on an interest in sex, violence or sensation? If so, does it matter?

Group discussions

Group 1 Should a private newspaper owner manipulate his editor to further his own interests and opinions? (Find out first which papers are personally owned.)

Group 2 How far should the press go in its coverage of the Royal Family? Give examples if you can, of fair reporting and unfair trespass.

Group 3 Should law breakers or scandal personalities be allowed to draw huge fees by giving interviews and life stories? How could this be stopped?

Group 4 How do you prefer to get news? Newspaper? (which one?) Radios 1, 2, 3 or 4? Local Radio? BBC TV? ITV? Channel 4?

Choose one member from each group to report back summarising your discussion, showing points of agreement and disagreement and solutions, if any.

Presenting a case from a newspaper

In the Certificate in Spoken English for Higher Education – an examination conducted by the English Speaking Board for Sixth Formers – the second section of the test is the presentation of a newspaper cutting of a topic on which the candidate has given considerable thought. (See page 175 in the appendices for detailed syllabus.)

1) The candidate presents the cutting to the assessor and then summarises the subject for the benefit of the listening participating group.

2) Having done that the candidate then shows his personal support or opposition.

3) The listeners ask questions and express their opinions which may be pro or con, or the assessor may invite two or three speakers to participate in a closer confrontation, especially if certain members of the listening group have opposite opinions. If it is a subject where there is agreement, there is still a place for contributive comment.

Some newspaper topics chosen by Sixth Formers presented in the English Speaking Board's Certificate in Spoken English for Higher Education.

1 Experiments on animals, especially with regard to beauty aids.
2 Beauty contests – a cattle market?
3 Glue sniffing – how to combat it.
4 Evictions begin at Greenham Common.
5 Laws relating to traffic offences (this particularly applies to the young people concerned as they are just becoming 'mobile').
6 Football hooliganism *on the pitch* (professional footballers setting an example to those on the terraces and what should happen to those who digress).
7 Fostering children (especially where coloured children are put with a white family).
8 Relations with the USSR.
9 Should the police be armed?
10 Shops complain about 'shoplifting' but are they not in a way responsible for the spread of this disease?
11 Is striking the best way for workers to obtain what they want?
12 Private education *v.* State education.
13 Working mothers? (inspired by article on court case where mother accused of neglecting children.)
14 Sportsmen paid too much? (inspired by article on transfer fees for footballers.)
15 Pollution of the countryside (spraying chemicals, pulling up hedges, motor fumes – what we can do about it).
16 Lead poisoning – from motor cars (what the car of the future should be like – how we can combat this disease, dangers all around us in many everyday things – child had died from lead poisoning).
17 Academic or vocational courses. Sixth-form confusion.
18 Two articles compared taking the pros and cons of experiments on animals:
    a) 'Needless cruelty' (*Daily Telegraph*)
    b) 'Wound tests on animals saved soldiers' lives' (*Daily Mail*)
19 Do you have to be wealthy to be healthy? (high prices in health shops.)
20 England to be expelled (Commonwealth Games).
21 Animal language (article on the BBC's programme).
22 Pre-marital sex experience (pros and cons).
23 The right to die (a cerebral palsy sufferer).
24 Queen's fury at Royal photos (harrassment in off-duty periods).
25 Dogs of war (dogs being trained as killers).
26 Spare-part surgery (an article written by a non-donor).
27 Persisting problem of the boat children (Vietnam refugees).

28 Political curbs extended for armed forces (changes in the Queen's regulations to stop service people participating in political demonstrations).
29 A question of rape – the jury's dilemma.
30 Fear over women priests (report on the Bishop of Birmingham).
31 Smear test for cervical cancer refused to women under 35 (women's magazine research reviewed in the *Daily Mail*).
32 Majority must be protected (report on the anti-smoking organisation ASH).
33 Why bother to vote? (a plea by an MP for people to accept the responsibility).
34 Lending money to Mexico.
35 The teachers' right to strike.
36 High Street purchasing of spectacles.
37 Public subsidy of the arts.
38 Whether or not the Elgin marbles should be sent to Greece.
39 The changing of Olympic rules regarding amateur status.
40 Buses should have conductors as well as drivers once again.
41 The rights and wrongs of leaking information to the press (by employees against employers).
42 Channel Tunnel – Partnered speakers –
    a) The folly of making a Channel Tunnel.
    b) The social, political and commercial value of the Channel Tunnel.
43 Should a political party ever take the side of one element in an industrial dispute?
44 Violence on television: who carries the responsibility?

A Background information

Before you put forward your case it would be as well to get to know rather more than the newspaper can present in its brief article. For example, if you have chosen a cutting which pleads for a rise in nurses' pay then try to get a few facts:

– Compare nurses' pay with that of other professions.
– Assess any 'perks' which may enhance the pay.
– Relate the salaries to years of training.
– Equate the salaries with the rate of inflation.
– Give examples which show the value of nurses' services to the community.

B Summarising your cutting

Paraphrase precisely not adding any emotional or persuasive words at this stage.

C Commenting on the article

If you are criticising the article then go for the weaknesses; if you are supporting the article now is the time to bring in your ammunition collected for (A).

D Answering questions and listening to comments

This is where your wider knowledge will quickly be tested. For instance, if your article was about seal culling you will need to know the different ways they are culled; how many make a viable colony; how many people are dependent on it for a living; the imbalance of food supplies and so on.

The assessor will determine the timing and pattern of the discussion and may intervene to put a question to the group.

What do the other newspapers say?

Is the paper from which you have taken your cutting biased? sensational? quick on giving news without investigation? or well considered?

It is a good exercise for groups to study different newspapers on any one day. (A newsagent would probably be able to save you one copy of several papers and let you have them cheap the day after. This must be pre-arranged as they have to account for and return unsold copies.)

Let us suppose that with your teacher's, school library and newsagent's support that you have managed to get one copy of each of the following:

GROUP 1 *The Times*; GROUP 2 *Guardian*; GROUP 3 *Daily Telegraph*; GROUP 4 *Daily Mail*; GROUP 5 *Daily Express*; GROUP 6 *Daily Mirror*; GROUP 7 *Sun*.

Study your group paper with these guidelines:

1) *Layout and lettering:*
Does the layout make the contents clear? Are there more pictures than words in large type? What is the range of sizes of letters – which words have the biggest space and why?

2) *Types of story:*
Is there any serious reporting of serious topics? Is the reporter interested in *all* the aspects of an event or topic? How many stories rely on 'human interest' as their main appeal? Does your newspaper have a sensible list of priorities when it gives most space to a particular issue? (Think about items of general importance in the world today, and compare the issues that other newspapers concentrate on.) Are some subjects done to death – e.g. the Royal Family?

3) *Foreign news:*
Is this only included for 'human interest' (i.e. the person involved just happens to be foreign – his background is irrelevant)? Is there anything to show the

paper's attitude to any foreign country? Does it deal in clichés – e.g. rich Americans, gloomy Russians, romantic Italians?

4) *Sports*:

How many pages are devoted to sport? Which sports are given most coverage? Does the paper examine any aspect of the sport beyond fixtures and personalities? (A couple of articles on the same football match would be helpful here.)

5) *Features*:

Which are informative and which are entertaining? Does the paper give too much space to TV celebrities and manufacture 'news' about them? Does it cater for any other special interests – gardening, travel, the arts, the Stock Exchange, collecting, etc.? Do these belong in a magazine, since they're not often news, in the sense of an important event newly discovered?

6) *Advertisements*:

Are these for ordinary consumer goods (like food) or expensive articles and services? Are jobs advertised and how are they presented? Is property advertised and what sort of income would a reader need to be interested in the property shown? Are personal advertisements or social events printed? Are any political meetings advertised?

7) *Style of vocabulary*:

Do the writers use normal paragraphs? Are the sentences brief or extended? What effect do these styles have on you? Is the language generally down-to-earth, abrupt or even violent? When you join the other groups compare two 'leader' articles to see how different editors talk to you – are they patronising or assuming that you are more stupid or well informed than you are?

8) *Photographs*:

Are the prints clear and the details well composed? Is the message of each one direct or producing a particular atmosphere (e.g. a soldier receiving an award for gallantry might be shown in smart uniform now, or in a grimy, tense state, as he was, when involved in a military operation)? Does a caption help the photographs? Are most photographs trying to show emotions or actions or both? Are there any where you feel the photographer has intruded on people's privacy?

Let each member of your group cover one of two of these headings.

Make notes to which you can refer when you join up with the other groups after a 15-minute study.

Each group then reports on its particular paper.

After these points have been noted and comparisons have been made, the groups could swap papers:

GROUP 1 *Sun*; GROUP 2 *Daily Mirror*; GROUP 3 *Daily Express*; GROUP 4 *The Times*; GROUP 5 *Guardian*; GROUP 6 *Daily Telegraph*; GROUP 7 *Daily Mail*.

In your group select a headline for each member to read aloud when the groups re-join.

Study quietly the correct emphasis and meaning. When you join up with the other groups the headlines should be announced with clarity and carrying power.

Choose one member from your group to do a half-minute commercial promotion on television to attract new readers. The composition of the words of the script will be a joint group effort. When the speaker addresses all the groups he will need to use persuasive vocal tone and facial expression.

Discuss the importance of any presentation of news of the following:

FAIRNESS,
CLARITY,
ACCURACY.

Keep these three qualities in mind and you will become a considerate listener and convincing speaker.

APPENDIX I   ASSESSMENT OF SPOKEN ENGLISH

As from 1988 when the new GCSE is introduced there is to be a compulsory oral component as part of the English paper. The National Criteria states that all GCSE syllabuses must include, as well as reading and writing, an oral communication test which is to be graded on a separate five-point scale. Awards will normally only be made to candidates who achieve a grade in both the written English papers and in oral communication.

The various boards, while all subscribing to the National Criteria as set out by the Secondary Examinations Council, have differing methods of assessment.

London and East Anglian Group: GCSE Oral Test

In the English Course there will be a compulsory separate assessment of oral communication skills, using teacher-assessed course work and a teacher-assessed test.

The English course is designed to develop spoken and written skills, together with responsiveness to, and enjoyment of, literature and other media. Oral communication will be internally assessed on a five-point scale, complementing the seven-point letter scale for written English which involves teacher-assessed work as well as an optional Board-assessed paper.

Throughout the course, students will be assessed on their competence in a range of spoken-language activities, taking into account content, interpersonal skills, language style and structure, and clarity of expression. The course will need to encourage responsive listening, clear speech, and a natural vocal vitality.

The separate oral assessments involve:

Oral Course Work – the size of groups will vary. For groups of three or more, activities might include formal or informal discussions on literary and non-literary texts, or media material; talks to large and small groups; role-play; scripted drama and improvisation. Preparatory work on an individual and pair basis is recommended, together with opportunities for *some* students to practice the reading aloud of passages of prose and verse.

Group Oral Test – this will take the form of five-minute discussions, involving five or six students, arising from a sequence of talks to be given by each for between three and four minutes. Candidates will be assessed by the class teacher and a second teacher from the same centre.

Candidates will be assessed for the communicative effectiveness of their performance, including eye contact with listeners, posture and gesture, pausing and timing, audibility and clarity.

Midland Examining Group: GCSE

English syllabus A includes an aural test requiring candidates to give written answers to spoken material played from a pre-recorded cassette. For both syllabuses A and B there is also a compulsory assessment during the course of oral communication skills, marked on a numerical scale by the teacher, and externally moderated. The emphasis is on the inter-relatedness of listening and speaking, and candidates are assessed on five group and/or individual speech activities. The following are given in the syllabus as examples only and are not intended to be prescriptive:

(a) a small group of discussion involving four to six candidates responding to a topic suggested by the group or teacher;
(b) a small group discussion on a subject introduced by a candidate who is to be assessed for the introductory talk/or chairing the meeting;
(c) group discussion from a given stimulus – e.g. drama, poetry, film, novel;
(d) a formal debate in which designated candidates would present their case;
(e) role-playing activities;
(f) reading aloud and play-reading;
(g) individual focussed talks on a prepared topic to a teacher or group of interested candidates;
(h) individual focussed conversation with a teacher;
(i) giving instructions to others for a task;
(j) reporting back;
(k) giving a description or relaying information from a visual or auditory source;
(l) giving an account of something learnt recently.

Candidates will be assessed on such factors as ability in:

– understanding and conveying information;
– ordering and presenting facts, ideas and opinions;
– evaluating what is heard, seen or read;
– describing and reflecting upon experience;
– presenting opinions and attitudes;
– responding appropriately to a particular audience;
– speaking audibly and intelligibly with a sense of appropriate tone, intonation and pace.

Southern Examining Group: GCSE Oral Test

In accordance with the National Criteria for GCSE English, the oral communication component of the Southern Examining Group's GCSE English syllabus must enable individual pupils to practise listening and speaking as inter-related skills within a broad range of experiences. Oral work should therefore play a fully integrated part in English.

While oral activity should arise naturally from and complement other aspects of work in English, so that talking and listening support reading and writing, the syllabus also recognises that the individual must be able to use language effectively for a number of different purposes and to a number of different audiences. The syllabus promotes this aim by suggesting three assessment categories:

(a) a situation involving two people in which both participants collaborate on a specified task;
(b) an open-ended group discussion;
(c) an exposition given by the candidate to an audience of one or more.

Category (c) is probably the one most in need of explanation since it is not explicitly included in the National Criteria. It is not the intention that all candidates should be forced to make formal speeches, although that option exists for those teachers and pupils who wish to use it. However, for practical reasons, some provision needs to be made to ensure that every candidate, even the shy and retiring, is heard to speak. It would surely be unfair on candidates whose contribution to group or pair discussion was slight, to assess them as lacking in ability when no clear obligation had been placed on them to talk. This requirement could be met quite simply, by asking an individual to report on his or her group discussion, for example.

Assessment is made on consideration of the four elements present in all language performance: the thinking involved, the language features (vocabulary and syntax), vocal quality (in the case of spoken language), and sensitivity to social context.

Northern Examining Association: GCSE

English Syllabuses A, B and C are designed to encourage an integrated approach to reading, writing, talking and listening. Oral communication will be *internally* assessed on a five-point numbered scale, according to the national criteria for English. (In English Syllabus C an *external* oral examination will be available for *external* candidates.)

In order to have a grade in English recorded on a certificate a candidate must also achieve at least Grade 5 in oral communication and in order to have a grade in oral communication recorded a candidate must also achieve Grade G in English.

Throughout the programme of English pupils are likely to attempt a wide variety of tasks with equally varied demands on their oral ability. Pupils will be directed towards producing a performance, such as a talk, a reading, a role play, a report, an interview, a narration of an anecdote, an explanation. Equally they will be involved in oral work arising from the context of other activities, such as exploring a poem or a story, discussing a topic, preparing a list of questions, brainstorming, preparing a statement of findings, solving a problem (simulation) or interviewing.

The oral assessment will relate to candidates' ability to:

(a) present and talk about information, imaginative work and what is read;
(b) select and evaluate evidence and present a point of view;
(c) discuss opinions or points of view;
(d) listen to others contributing and respond showing understanding and appreciation of what is said;
(e) describe and communicate what has been experienced, felt or imagined;
(f) interact with others and respond appropriately in different contexts.

These skills are not likely to be entirely separable, but on any one occasion assessment may focus on particular abilities. It is essential that candidates participate in a sufficiently varied programme to enable assessment of the above range of abilities.

Candidates will be assessed for their use of appropriate register, vocabulary, idiom, intonation, pace, tone, gesture. The assessment will take account of their ability to listen to others with empathy, discuss the nature and qualities of what is being said, and respond sensitively and constructively.

Welsh Joint Education Committee: GCSE Oral Test

Oral communication will be assessed throughout the GCSE course. Careful organisation will be required to enable candidates to show their ability in talking and listening in situations which form a natural part of classroom activity.

The overall aims of the English course relate to writing with a clearly defined purpose, organising ideas in rational sequence to relate to both content and audience awareness, and using language effectively and accurately. Oral communication skill is related to these requirements through the practice of formal and semi-formal speech, involving the following activities:

Formal:
Group discussion with formal framework for specific task/issue, using a chairman.
Report to whole class on outcome of group discussion.
Prepared talk to whole class on hobby or interest, followed by questions.
Introduction and reading of prepared passage, followed by questions from class.
Debate.
Simulation of formal interview (e.g. for job) – pupil/pupil or pupil/teacher.

Semi-formal:
Group discussion, semi-formal style, with a variety of stimuli and topics.
Improvised acting situations.
One-to-one conversation arising from candidate's project or topic of interest.
Contribution to class discussions.

An overall impression mark will be awarded for the two aspects of oral communication indicated above, taking into account appropriate command of language; content and ideas; physical use of voice; listening with understanding; and awareness of audience.

Scottish Standard Grade

English on the Standard Grade requires the assessment and moderation of 'talking', which will be taught and developed throughout the course with internal summative assessment and external moderation on a seven-point scale with related grade criteria.

Pupils will be assessed during their course on a variety of speech situations, ranging from the informality of conversation to the rule-bound requirements of debating speech. Oral communication is emphasised both as the main means of relating to others and as a way of acquiring and ordering ideas.

Five purposes for talk are specified:

– to convey information;
– to deploy ideas, expound, argue, evaluate;
– to describe personal experiences, express feeling and reactions;
– to create particular effects;
– to work in a group towards a common goal.

Three situations are stipulated in which talk can be developed:

(a) *one-to-one talk* – involving interview, discussion, conversation;
(b) *solo talk to an audience* – reporting back after discussion, contributing as a member of a panel, symposium, or debating team, giving a short talk, or telling a story;
(c) *group participation* – with or without a designated leader but with pre-determined remit.

Note (i): functional role-play can be used when appropriate. 'This is not to be confused with play-acting or theatrical presentation . . .' but should relate to a pupil adopting a role, for example, as editor of a newspaper chairing a community meeting, or a representative of a charity addressing an appeal to an audience.

Note (ii): telephone skills can be demonstrated for one-to-one talk.

Pupils will be assessed on:

(a) intelligibility – meaning, voice, speech, delivery;
(b) appropriateness to purpose – ideas, language, awareness, structure;
(c) aspects of purpose – five factors previously mentioned above.

The English Speaking Board

This independent board is concerned with the teaching and assessing of spoken English throughout school and college life and into vocational and professional adult training. To cover this wide range from early primary through the secondary stage to various sectors of vocational training it has a series of syllabuses and certificates finely geared to give individual candidates scope to relate their oral presentations to their personal skills and interests.

The Senior syllabuses (covering the 12–18 age group) are based on the following tests:

(a) a personal project which can include documentary and graphic visual material and demonstration apparatus;
(b) own choice of interpretative literature (poetry, prose, drama; solo or group);
(c) own choice pre-studied book from which the assessor chooses a short passage for reading aloud;
(d) meeting the situation: answers to questions from the group discussion or role-playing.

In all ESB assessments the listening, participating group are an essential part of the procedure and candidates area assessed throughout the session on their listening and response.

The other assessments which are of special interest to the 16–18 age group in schools and further education are: (a) the Pre-Vocational Syllabus (devised for candidates going into vocational training), and (b) the Certificate in Spoken English for Higher Education (devised for students in the sixth form going on to Higher Education). The former includes telephoning techniques and the latter the presentation of a newspaper cutting leading to group discussion

Syllabuses, together with detailed guidelines on teaching and assessing, will be sent on request to the English Speaking Board, 32 Norwood Avenue, Southport.

The following boards now also have an oral communication component in some of their syllabuses:

Associated Board of the Royal Schools of Music
  14 Bedford Square, London, WC1H 0PX

Chamber of Commerce
  69 Cannon Street, London, EC4

City and Guilds of London Institute
  76 Portland Place, London, W1N 4AA

College of Preceptors
  Coppice Row, Theydon Bois, Epping, Essex, CM16 7DN

Guildhall School of Music and Drama
  The Barbican, London, EC2Y 8DT

LAMDA
  Tower House, 226 Cromwell Road, London, SW5

Royal Society of Arts
  6–8 Adam Street, London, WC2N 6EZ

APPENDIX II   SELECTED BIBLIOGRAPHY AND RESOURCE MATERIAL

Books for teachers of oral skills

GCSE Criteria: English GCSE, A Guide for Teachers (Secondary Examinations Council, OUP 1985).

Creative Oral Assessment: A handbook for teachers and assessors of Spoken English: Christabel Burniston (English Speaking Board 1983).

For language across the curriculum: *A Language for Life:* (Bullock Report HMSO) especially pp. 115–38; 141–61.

Language, Schools and Classrooms: Michael Stubbs (2nd edition, Methuen 1983).

Advanced Work in English: C.R.E. Parker (a book for 6th formers) (Longman 1982).

Teaching Talk: strategies for production and assessment: Gillian Brown, Anne Anderson, Richard Shillock and George Yule (Cambridge University Press 1985).

Better Schools: (HMSO 1985), especially pp. 2, 7 (para. 25), 15 (para. 3), 16 (para. 49), 29 (para. 92), 30 (para. 96), 41 (para. 134), 42 (para. 136).

Education 16–19: The role of English and communication: J. Brown (Macmillan).

Voice and speech techniques

Voice Production and Speech: Greta Colson (Museum Press 1963).

Voice and the Actor: Cicely Berry (Harrap 1973).

Instant Eloquence: Public speaking made easy: James C Hume (London Barnes & Noble 1985).

Speak with Confidence: John Holgate and David Coulter
  Based on the London TV series 'I say') (Stanley Paul 1974).

Telephoning

Leta publications are available in a loose-leaf worksheet format designed for photocopying. The price includes permission.

Be Confident about Using the Telephone: Part 1: worksheet or booklet.
Basic Phone Scripts: supplement to Part 1 with role-playing dialogue.
Be Confident about Using the Telephone: Part II worksheet or booklet.

(All Leta publications and price-lists are obtainable from: ESB, 32 Norwood Avenue, Southport)

Student course books for spoken English (16 +)

Network One (An English course book for upper secondary school pupils):
Keith Hurse and John Sims (Hodder & Stoughton 1981).
Appropriate English: (Books 1–4) Richard Adams, John L Foster and Robert
L Wilson (Book 4 would be appropriate for the 16+) (Macmillan 1984).
Speech for Life: Christabel Burniston (there are a few copies of the final 6th
Australian printing, 1982, available from ESB) (originally published by
Pergamon Press, 1968).
Spoken English in Advanced Education: Christabel Burniston (a course book
for mature students) (English Speaking Board 1974).
Be Confident about Giving a Talk: Louise Estill.
Be Confident about Reading Aloud: Louise Estill.

The last two give step-by-step guidance in book form or worksheets with
permission to photocopy (obtainable from ESB office or direct from: Louise
Estill, 15 Kingsway, Gerrards Cross, Bucks SL9).

Film and video

Many stage plays, TV plays and documentaries are now published for general
distribution on colour video tapes. The British Theatre Association has an
excellent library of plays. Useful addresses for information:

Record Ridgeway Education Service, Parkway Works Sheffield, S9 3BL
Hargreaves Audio-Visual Department, 204–232 Warbreck Moor, Aintree,
Liverpool 9
Society for Education in Films and Television, 29 Old Compton Street,
London, W1V 5PL
British Theatre Association, 9 Fitzroy Square, London W1P 6AE

Organisations to help the 16 + students professionally and socially

National Federation of Young Farmers Clubs, YFC Centre, National
Agricultural Centre, Kenilworth, Warwickshire
Outward Bound Trust, Avon House, 360 Oxford Street, London W1N 9HA
Royal Jubilee Trust, 8 Buckingham Street, London WC2N 6BU
Voluntary Service Overseas, 9 Belgrave Square, London SW1 8PW
Youth Hostels Association, Trevelyan House, St Albans, Hertfordshire AL1
2DY
National Union of Students, 3 Endsleight Street, London WC1H 0DU
Young Men's Christian Association, 640 Forest Road, London E17 3DZ

Organisations and charities which have useful background and reference material for projects; themes; discussion, debates and appeals. The names of other charities and their specific objectives can be found in *Charities Digest*: a publication of the Family Welfare Association.

Oxfam, 274 Banbury Road, Oxford OX2 7DZ, and local branches
Afasic (speech-impaired children), 347 Central Market, Smithfield, London EC1A 9NH
NSPCC, 1–3 Riding House Street, London W1P 8AA
RSPCA, Causeway, Horsham, West Sussex
Save the Children Fund, 157 Clapham Road, London SW9 0PT
Age Concern, 60 Pitcairn Road, Milcham, Surrey
British Red Cross Society, 9 Grosvenor Crescent, London SW1
Child Poverty Action Groups, 1 Macklin Street, London WC2B 5NH
Keep Britain Tidy, Bostel House, 37 West Street, Brighton BN1

Local voluntary organisations which support youth projects and/or supply information and guidance:

Rotary Clubs of Great Britain, Sheen Lane House, Sheen Lane, London SW14 8AF
Round Tables (local directories)
Soroptomists, 63 Bayswater Road, London W2 3PJ
Business and Professional Women's Clubs (local directories)
Womens Institutes (local directories)
Townswomen's Guilds, National Union of Townswomen's Guilds, 2 Cromwell Place, London SW7 2JG
Citizens Advice Bureau (local directories)
Samaritans (local directories)
Local radio (*Radio Times* and local directories)

(If the addresses cannot be found in your local directory, your reference library or publicity department will have the name and address of the local secretary and the venues for the meetings.)

ACKNOWLEDGMENTS

The authors are indebted to the many schools and colleges whose projects and skills are quoted in this book, and to the thousands of students and candidates who have used 'direct speech' in classwork and oral assessments. In particular we are grateful for being observers and participants in the English Speaking Board courses, classes and assessments and for the cooperation of students and tutorial staff of King George Vth Sixth Form College.

We should also like to thank the various GCSE boards for their willingness to share and discuss their syllabuses for the oral section of their English syllabuses and cooperating with Kenneth Hastings, Director of the English Speaking Board, in summarising the various syllabuses. We are indebted to Kenneth Hastings for the resultant contribution to appendix 1.

The authors would also like to record their appreciation of Margaret Edwards of Westholme School, Blackburn, who provided a great deal of material on newspaper projects from which we selected items for Section 3 of Chapter 10. Pressure of space made it impossible to do justice to her research and teaching expertise in this subject. Some of the drama exercises in Dialogue in Action were inspired by Ken Googe, Drama Adviser for Wigan MBC and Vita Milne of Cambridge.

The authors and publishers would like to thank the following for their kind permission to reproduce copyright texts: David Higham Associates Ltd for an extract from *Akenfield* by Ronald Blythe; Gower Publishing for an extract from *Working* by Studs Terkel; The Bodley Head and the Estate of Henry Williamson for an extract from *Tarka the Otter* by Henry Williamson; Collins Publishers for 'Inexpensive Progress' by John Betjeman from *Poems 1930–45* and for 'My Father's Skill' by Camara Laye from *The Dark Child*; Oxford University Press for 'Behaviour of Money' reprinted from Bernard Spencer's *Collected Poems*, edited by Roger Bowen (1981); André Deutsch Ltd for 'Roads' and 'The Tower Block' by Michael Rosen from *Wouldn't You Like to Know*; David Higham Associates Ltd and J. M. Dent Ltd for 'Memories of Christmas' by Dylan Thomas from *Child's Christmas in Wales*; Jonathan Cape Ltd for an extract from *Catch 22* by Joseph Heller; Austin-Rover Group Ltd for an extract from the Austin-Rover Triumph Acclaim Handbook; Faber & Faber Ltd for 'A Constable Calls' by Seamus Heaney from *North* and for 'One fine day on the beach' by Alan Bennett from *The Writer in Disguise*; John Johnson (Author's Agency) Ltd for an extract from *The Golden Horseshoe* by Patrick Duggan; Methuen London for 'Mixed Doubles' from *Countdown* by Alan Ayckbourn, and for an extract from *Antigone* by Jean Anouilh, translated by Lewis Galantiere; Olwyn Hughes for an extract from *Orpheus* by Ted Hughes, copyright © Ted Hughes. First published by BBC Publications; Community Service Volunteers for 'Greenham District Council Role-Play Games' by Ken Jones; and Ben Mkapa for his poem 'Facing a Volcano'; Hamish Hamilton Ltd and Rosemary A. Thurber for the parable 'The Last Flower' by James Thurber copyright © 1939 James Thurber, copyright © 1967 Helen Thurber and Rosemary Thurber, published by Harper and Rowe.

We should be grateful for any information which may help us trace the copyright holder of 'The Battle of Jericho' by Valerie Lishman.

For permission to use photographs the authors and publishers wish to thank: Sally and Richard Greenhill (pp. 3, 16, 35, 37, 46, 78 and 149); the National Film Archive (pp. 24, 84, 145 and 147); W. P. F. Mason of the Solihull Education and Training Centre (pp. 31 and 73); Stamford Photographic Services (p. 100); Alma Rafter of Berkhamsted School for Girls (pp. 104 and 107); David Scott of Chatham Grammar School (p. 102); and *Solihull News* (p. 105).